Little Red Book of SMS Language

Chat Room Slang

By the same author:

Treasure Chest for Public Speaking

Little Red Book Series

Little Red Book of English Vocabulary
Little Red Book of Grammar Made Easy
Little Red Book of Euphemisms
Little Red Book of English Proverbs
Little Red Book of Idioms & Phrases
Little Red Book of Acronyms and Abbreviations
Little Red Book of Modern Writing Skills
Little Red Book of Effective Speaking Skills

A2Z Book Series

A2Z Quiz Book
A2Z Book of Word Origins

Fiction

Vilayti Pani: The Anglo-Indian Novel

Little Red Book of SMS Language
Chat Room Slang

Terry O'Brien

Rupa & Co

Copyright © Terry O'Brien 2011

Published 2011 by
Rupa Publications India Pvt. Ltd.
7/16, Ansari Road, Daryaganj,
New Delhi 110 002

Sales Centres:
Allahabad Bengaluru Chennai
Hyderabad Jaipur Kathmandu
Kolkata Mumbai

All rights reserved.
No part of this publication may be reproduced, stored in a retrieval system, or transmitted, in any form or by any means, electronic, mechanical, photocopying, recording or otherwise, without the prior permission of the publishers.

The author asserts the moral right to be identified as the author of this work

Typeset by
Anvi Composers
19, A1-B, DDA Market
Paschim Vihar
New Delhi 110 063

Printed in India by
Shree Maitrey Printech Pvt. Ltd.
A-84, Sector-2
Noida-201301

To all SMS buffs!
SMS Language is like adolescence-the awkward age when a child is too old to say something cute and too bound to say something sensible

Terry O'Brien

Warning: SMS language as "wrecking our language."

PREFACE

The rise of technology has brought about the advent of a lot of things that has changed the way we view and live our lives today. So also, the way we look at communication. Now there's no need to email or to even call your friends. With the development of SMS, things never have become so much easier. OBE stands for 'Overcome By Events.' The number 114 is the number shorthand for information. It is so addictive and compelling in nature that it has even created its own version of the English language. This sub-language is known for its expressiveness using emoticons as well as its economy due to its use of several abbreviations. The Red Book of SMS Language puts together a complete list of SMS linguistics for its users and readers. So Enjoy!.

tob... Terry O'Brien

USE CHARACTERS AND THEIR MEANINGS

&	and
0	nothing
2	two, to, too
2DAY	today
A	a / an
B	be
B4	before
BC	because
BF	boyfriend
BK	back
BRO	brother
BT	but
C	see
D8	date
DNR	dinner
EZ	easy
F8	fate
GF	girlfriend
GR8	great
HOLS	holidays
HV	have
I	I, it
Its	it is
KDS	kids
L8	late
L8R	later
M8	mate

NE1	anyone
PLS	please
PS	parents
QT	cutie
R	are
SIS	sister
SKOOL	school
SMMR	summer
U	you
WR	were
A3	anyplace, anytime, anywhere
ASAP	as soon as possible
B4N	Bye for now
BAU	business as usual
BRB	I'll be right back.
BTW	by the way
CUL	see you later
CWOT	complete waste of time
FTF	face to face
FYI	for your information
GMTA	great minds think alike
HAND	have a nice day
HRU	how are you
ICBW	it could be worse
IDTS	I don't think so
IMHO	in my humble opinion
IYKWIM	if you know what I mean
JK	just kidding
KOTC	kiss on the cheek

LOL	laughing out loud
LSKOL	long slow kiss on the lips
LTNS	long time no see
Luv U	I love you.
Luv U2	I love you too.
MON	the middle of nowhere
MTE	my thoughts exactly
MU	I miss you.
MUSM	I miss you so much.
NP	no problem
OIC	oh, I see
PC&QT	peace and quiet
PCM	please call me
ROTFL	rolling on the floor laughing
RUOK	are you ok?
THNQ	thank you
U4E	you forever
UROK	you are okay
WUCIWUG	what you see is what you get
WYSIWYG	what you see is what you get
XLNT	excellent
:-*	kiss
)	very happy
:0	shocked
:")	blushing
<:3)~	mouse
:@)	pig
:')	tears of laughter
***)**	stick tongue out

x	you make me sick
:"	whistling
:@	screaming
O	saintly

BASIC A TO Z OF SMS LINGO

A

AAM	As a matter of fact.
AB	Ah Bless!
ADctd2uv	Addicted to Love
AFAIK	As far as I know
AKA	Also known as
ALlWanIsU	All I want is You
AML	All my love
ASAP	As soon as possible
ATB	All the best
ATW	At the weekend
AWHFY	Are we having fun yet

B

B4	Before
BBFN	Bye Bye for now.
BBS	Be back soon
BBSD	Be back soon darling
BCNU	Be seein' you
BF	Boy friend
BGWM	Be gentle with me

BRB	Be right back
BTW	By the way

C

Cld9?	Cloud 9 ?
Cm	Call me
Cu	See you
CUIMD	See you in my dreams
Cul	See you later
CUL8R	See you later

D

Dk	Don't know
Dur?	Do you remember?

E

E2eg	Ear to ear grin
EOD	End of discussion
EOL	End of lecture

F

F?	Friends
F2F	Face to face
F2T	Free to talk
FITB	Fill in the Blank
FYEO	For your eyes only
FYA	For your amusement
FYI	For your information

G

GF	Girl friend.
GG	Good game
GMeSumLuvin	Give me some lovin'!
Gr8	Great
GSOH	Good salary, own home
GTSY	Glad to see you

H

h2cus	Hope to see you soon
H8	Hate
HAGN	Have a good night
HAND	Have a nice day
HldMeCls	Hold me close
H&K	Hugs and Kisses

I

IDK	I don't know
IGotUBabe	I've got you babe
IIRC	If I recall correctly
IMHO	In my humble opinion
IMI	I mean it
ILU	I love You
IMBLuv	It must be love
IOW	In other words
IOU	I owe you
IUSS	If you say so

J

J4F	Just for fun
JFK	Just for kicks
JstCllMe	Just call me

K

KC	Keep cool
KHUF	Know how you feel
KIT	Keep in touch
KOTC	Kiss on the cheek
KOTL	Kiss on the lips

L

L8	Late
L8r	Later
Lol	Laughing out loud
LTNC	Long time no see
LtsGt2gthr	Let's get together

M

M$ULkeCrZ	Miss you like crazy!
M8	Mate
MC	Merry christmas
MGB	May God Bless
Mob	Mobile
MYOB	Mind your own business

N

NA	No access
NC	No comment
NE	Any
NE1	Anyone
No1	No-one
NWO	No way out

O

O4U	Only for you
OIC	Oh, I see
OTOH	On the other hand

P

PCM	Please call me
PPL	People

Q

QT	Cutie

R

R	Are
RMB	Ring my bell
ROTFL	Roll on the floor laughing
RU?	Are you?
RUOK?	Are you OK?

S

SC	Stay cool
SETE	Smiling ear to ear
SO	Significant other
SOL	Sooner or later
SME1	Some one
SRY	Sorry
SWALK	Sent with a loving kiss
SWG	Scientific wild guess

T

T+	Think positive
T2ul	Talk to you later
TDTU	Totally devoted to you
Thx	Thanks
T2Go	Time to go
TIC	Tongue in cheek
TTFN	Ta ta for now.

U

U	You
UR	You are
URT1	You are the one

V

VRI	Very

W

W4u	Waiting for you
WAN2	Want to
WLUMRyMe	Will you marry me?
WRT	With respect to
WUWH	Wish you were here

X

X!	Typical woman
X	Kiss
XclusvlyUrs	Exclusively yours

Y

Y!	Typical Man
YBS	You'll be Sorry

Z

ZZZ	Sleeping

CHAT, E-MAIL, WEB, AND CHAT ROOM SLANG AND ACRONYMS

AAK	Alive and kicking
AAR	At any rate
AAS	Alive and smiling
ADN	Any day now
AFAIK	As far as I know
AFK	Away from the keyboard
AFN	That's all for now
AOTA	All of the above
a/s/l or asl	Age/Sex/Location - (used to ask a chatter their personal information)
AV	Avatar - Graphical representation (a picture) often used in chat rooms to depict a person that is in the room and chatting.
b4	Before
BAK	Back at keyboard (I'm back)
BBL	Be back later
BBS	Be back soon
BCNU	I'll be seeing you
b/f	Boyfriend (also shown as bf, B/F, or BF)
BEG	Big evil grin
BFN	Bye for now

Boot	To get kicked out of a chat room, or have to restart the computer because you couldn't talk in the chat room anymore.
BR	Best regards
BRB	Be right back
BRH	Be right here
BTA	But then again....
BTW	By the way
btw	Between you and me ...
Chat room	A web page where people gather using software that allows them to talk to one another in real time.
CU	See you - also posted as CYA
CNP	Continued in next post (seen more on message boards than chat)
CP	Chat post
CUL8R	See you later
CUOL	See you on line
CYA	See ya
dd, ds, dh	Darling or dear: dear son, dear daughter, or dear husband. Usually exchanged in family chats.
DEGT	Don't even go there (I don't want to talk about it)
DIKU	Do I know you?
DIS	Did I Say

D/L, DL, d/l, dl	Downloading, or Download it.
EG	Evil grin
EM	E-mail
EMA	E-mail Address (example: ?ema or ema? = what is your email address)
EOT	End Of thread (meaning end of discussion)
ez or EZ	Easy (one of the really old ones)
F2F	Face To Face
FAQ	Frequently Asked Question
FISH	First In Still Here (someone who is on line TOO much)
FITB	Fill In The Blanks
Flame	To insult someone. Used when a person asks a stupid question, or says something rude to irritate the users of a chat room or message board.
FOCL	Falling Off Chair - Laughing
forum	What todays message boards are called. Often using PHP as defining language to quickly write 'real time' messages and replies to a web site (or page)
FUBAR	"Fouled" Up Beyond All Repair / Recognition
FUD	Fear, Uncertainty, and Doubt

FWIW	For What It's Worth
FYI	For Your Information
GA	Go Ahead
GAL	Get a Life
Gest	Gesture ... a small multimedia file played over the internet, usually expressing an emotion or comment.
G/F	Girlfriend (also shown as gf, G/F, or GF)
GFN	Gone For Now
GGOH	Gotta get outta here
GMTA	Great Minds Think Alike
GR	Gotta run
GR&D	Grinning, Running, and Ducking.
GTR	Got to run
GTRM	Going to Read Mail (leaving chat room to check email)
H&K	Hugs and Kisses
Hack	Person who breaks into software, or disrupts a chat room.
HAGD	Have a Good Day
HAGO	Have a good one
HB	Hurry Back
Hosts	Refers to the people that are running the chat room, they usually have the ability to kick a person off due to rude behavior

HTH	Hope That Helps
Huggles	Hugs
IAC	In Any Case
IB	I'm Back
IC	I See
IDN	I don't know
IDK	I don't know
IDTS	I don't think So
IANAL	I Am Not A Lawyer (expect an uninformed opinion)
IC	I see
ICQ	I Seek You. A computer program used to communicate instantly over the Internet.
ILU or ILY	I Love You
IM	Instant Message
IMHO	In My Humble Opinion (or In My Honest Opinion)
IMO	In my Opinion
IOH	I'm out of here
IOW	In other Words
IRL	In Real Life
IYO	In Your Opinion
JAS	Just A Second
JIC	Just In Case
JK	Just Kidding
JMO	Just My Opinion
JW	Just Wondering
k, K, or kk	O. K.
KIT	Keep In Touch

L8R	Later (an early one, kind of outdated with current 'young geeks')
LOL	Laughing Out Loud
LTNS	Long Time No See
LTS	Laughing To oneself
LY	I Love Ya
LYL	Love You Lots
Message Board.	A web page where people write comments, and those comments are then added to that webpage for others to view. Used to carry on conversation, request information, and relay messages.
MUG	Refers to a new user of that chat programme,? goes back to Excite VP days when the AV (or icon) that represented someone new was a picture of a coffee mug.
NE1	Anyone
Newbie	Refers to a person who is new to an area or technology. Also seen as nube, nooby, nubie, nb, etc.
NIMBY	Not In My Back Yard
nm, or NM	Never Mind
NP, np	No Problem

NRN	No Response Necessary/ Not Right Now
NT	No Thanks
OBTW	Oh, by the way
OIC	Oh, I See
OJ or OK	Only Joking or Only Kidding
OL	The Old Lady
OM	The Old Man
OMG	Oh My Gosh
OT	Off Topic
oth or OTH	Off The Hook: Something is really popular, or hot. Very exciting.
otr or OTR	Off The Rack: Saying that something is outside the ordinary.
OTE	Over The Edge (beyond common sense or beyond good taste)
OTOH	On The Other Hand ...
OTOMH	Off the Top of My Head ...
OTW	On The Way ... I've sent a file to you, it's "On the way"
P911	My parents are in the room. P=Parents, and 911=emergency, in other words either drop the subject, or watch the language.
PANS	Pretty Awesome New Stuff (often referring to computer technology)

PCMCIA	Personal Computer Memory Cards International Association
PCMCIA	People Can't Master Computer Industry Acronyms (slang)
PEBCAK	Problem Exists Between Chair And Keyboard
Peeps	People. example: "There sure are a lot of peeps in this room" - meaning a lot of people are in the chat room.
Peep this	Hey, listen to this, I've got some interesting news.
PLZ	Please
PMJI	Pardon Me for Jumping In (when you enter into a new conversation)
Poof	When someone leaves a chat room, often seen as *poof* as in: Boy he *poofed* in a hurry.
POTS	Plain Old Telephone Service
POS	Parents are looking over my Shoulder.
POTS	Parents over the Shoulder - (My parents are watching, I can't really talk)
PPL	People
QT	Cutie

RFC	Request for Comments (used more in newsgroups, a page or pages that supply technical information)
rl or RL	Real Life (as opposed to being online)
r m or RM	Ready Made: pre-existing
ROFL	Rolling On Floor, Laughing
ROTF	Rolling On The Floor (laughing is implied)
RSN	Real Soon Now
r/t	Real Time (also: RT, or rt)
RTFM	Read The "Flippin" Manual (response to beginner question on net, chat, newsgroups, etc.)
RU	Are you?
SH	Same Here
SN	Screen Name. The name or moniker selected by a person in an IM or chat programme. ex: My "SN" in vp was "-lone.wolf"
SNAFU	Situation Normal, All "Fouled" Up
SO	Significant Other
SOTA	State Of The Art (latest technology)
SPST	Same Place, Same Time
STW	Search the Web
SY	Sincerely Yours
SYL	See You Later

TAFN	That's all for now
TC	Take Care
TFH	Thread from Hell (a topic or discussion that won't stop - esp. newsgroups)
TGIF	Thank Goodness It's Friday
THX	Thanks!
TIA	Thanks In Advance
TM	Text Message (often refers to communications with text over cell phones)
TMI	Too Much Info. (information)
TNT	Til Next Time
TPS	That's Pretty Stupid
TPTB	The Powers That Be (can sometimes refer to the people that are running the chat room or server)
TRDMF	Tears Running Down My Face: Can be with either laughter, or due to sadness.
TTFN	Ta-Ta For Now
TTTT	These Things Take Time
TTYL	Talk To You Later
TY	Thank You
TYT	Take Your Time
TYVM	Thank You Very Much
VPPH	Virtual Places Page Host

usa or USA	Until Sides Ache: Usually used with one of the laughter acronyms such as "lolusa" Laughing Out Loud Until my Sides Ache.
UV	Unpleasant visual
UW	You're Welcome
vp or VP	Virtual Places: A brand of chat offered by Excite in the late 90s and early 2000.
WB	Welcome Back (you say this when someone returns to a chat room)
WC	Welcome
WEG	Wicked Evil Grin
WEU	What's Eating You?
WFM	Works For Me
WIIFM	What's In It For Me?
WTG	Way To Go
WTGP?	Want To Go Private? (move to a private chat room)
YAA	Yet Another Acronym
YBS	You'll Be Sorry
YL	Young Lady
YM	Young Man
YMMV	Your Mileage May Vary
YR	Yea, Right (sarcastic)
YVW	You're Very Welcome
YW	You're Welcome

EMOTICONS

Emoticons are symbols used to display feeling. For these little things called "emoticons" often the idea is to turn your head sideways, and it makes a picture on a lot of the smiley faces. ;-) for example where the ; (semi-colon) are the eyes, the - is the nose, and the) is the mouth. Also, you see some people use the hyphen (-) to show the nose, while others will show the same expression without the nose. Example: ;-) and ;) signify the same thing.

s, *S*, <s>,	Smile
g, <g>	Grin
xoxo	Hugs and kisses
hugggggggsssss	Hugs
w, <w>	Wink
g,	Giggles
k, *K*	Kiss
(((((person)))))	Giving them a virtual hug.
\~/	Glass with a drink (usually booze)
^5	High five
?^	What's Up?
_/?	A cup of tea
[_]> +	Cup of coffee
@@@	Cookies
@--/	A rose
:-)	Smile
;-)	Wink
<:-|	Curious

:~)	Cute
:-(	Sad
8-)	Wears glasses
:-}	Embarrassed
:-/	Perplexed, confused
-(.	To cry
:-<	Pouting
>:-(	Angry
0:-)	Angel
:-|	Bored or no opinion
:->	Grin/mischievous
|-)	Dreaming
:-O	Shouting, or shocked
:-o	Talking, or surprised
>:-||	Mad / angry
:-D	Big grin or laugh
=:-O	Scared
:-x	Keeping mouth shut
:o)	Smiles (w/nose)
:-)))))))	Lots of smiles
;-P	Sticking tongue out
:P	Sticking tongue out
#8-)	Nerd, or person with glasses and crew cut
&-(	Crying
!:-)	I have an idea
;-{)	Person with a moustache
;~)	Being cute
c["]	Coffee mug

_]>	Another cup or mug
:->	Grin/mischievous
<:-|	Curious
|-|	Sound asleep
:-x	I'm keeping my mouth shut

LOVER'S ACRONYMS

SWALK Sealed with a loving kiss

SWALKCAKWS Sealed with a lick 'cos a kiss won't stick

BOLTOP Better on lips than on paper

ILUVM I l love you very much

ITALY I trust and love you

HOLLAND here our love lies and never dies

INTERNET SLANG

Internet Slang is also called AOL speak, AOLese, AOLbonics, netspeak, or leetspeak. While it does save keystrokes, netspeak can prove very hard to read. Internet slang has become widely used.

Here is a list of email, instant message and chat room acronyms (slang) and word abbreviations commonly used online - and their meanings:

A to Z and more ...

A

AAMOF	As a matter of fact
ABFL	A big fat lady
ABT	About
ADDY (ADDYS - plural)	Address
ADN	Any day now
AFAIC	As far as I'm concerned
AFAICT	As far as I can tell
AFAICS	As far as I can see
AFAIK	As far as I know
AFAYC	As far as you're concerned
AFK	Away from keyboard
AISI	As I see it
AIUI	As I understand it
AKA	Also known as
AML	All my love
ANFSCD	And now for something completely different
ASAP	As soon as possible
ASL	Assistant section leader
ASL	Age, sex, location
ASLP	Age, sex, location, picture
A/S/L	Age/sex/location
ASOP	Assistant system operator
ATM	At this moment
AWA	As well as
AWHFY	Are we having fun yet?

AWGTHTGTTA	Are we going to have to go through this again?
AWOL	Absent without leave
AWOL	Away without leave
AYOR	At your own risk
AYPI?	And your point is?

B

B4	Before
B4N	Bye for now
BAC	Back at computer
BAK	Back at the keyboard
BBIAB	Be back in a bit
BBL	Be back later
BBLBNTSBO...	Be back later but not too soon because of...
BBR	Burnt beyond repair
BBS	Be back soon
BBS	Bulletin board system
BC	Be cool
B/C	Because
BCnU	Be seeing you
BEG	Big evil grin
BF	Boyfriend
B/F	Boyfriend
BFN	Bye for now
BG	Big grin
BIH	Burn In Hell
BION	Believe it or not

BIOYIOB	Blow it out your I/O port
BITMT	But in the meantime
BMTIPG	Brilliant minds think in parallel gutters
BKA	Better known as
BL	Belly laughing
BOL	Be on later
BOT	Back on topic
BRB	Be right back
BRBS	Be right back soon
BRH	Be right here
BRS	Big red switch
BS	Big smile
BSF	But seriously folks
BST	But seriously though
BTA	But then again
BTAIM	Be that as it may
BTDT	Been there done that
BTOBD	Be there or be dead
BTOBS	Be there or be square
BTW	By the way
BUDWEISER	Because you deserve what every individual should ever receive
BWQ	Buzz word quotient
BWTHDIK	But what the heck do I know
BYOB	Bring your own bottle
BYOH	Bat You Onna Head
B&	Banned

C

C&G	Chuckle and grin
CAD	Ctrl-alt-delete
CADET	Can't add, doesn't even try
CDIWY	Couldn't do it without you
CD9	Code 9 - parents are around
CFV	Call for votes
CFS	Care for secret?
CFY	Calling for you
CID	Crying in disgrace
CLM	Career limiting move
CM@TW	Catch me at the web
CMIIW	Correct me if I'm wrong
CNP	Continue in next post
CO	Conference
CSG	Chuckle snicker grin
CTS	Changing the subject
CU	See you
CU2	See you too
CUL	See you later
CUL8R	See you later
CWOT	Complete waste of time
CWYL	Chat with you later
CYA	See ya
CYAL8R	See ya later
CYO	See you online

D

DBA	Doing business as
DCed	Disconnected
DFLA	Disenhanced four-letter acronym
DH	Darling husband
DIIK	Darn if I know
DGA	Digital guardian angel
DIKU	Do I know you?
DIRTFT	Do it right the first time
DITYID	Did I tell you I'm distressed
DIY	Do it yourself
DL	Download
DL	Dead link
DLTBBB	Don't let the bed bugs bite
DMMGH	Don't make me get hostile
DQMOT	Don't quote me on this
DND	Do not disturb
DTC	Darn this computer
DTRT	Do the right thing
DUCT	Did you see that?
DWAI	Don't worry about it
DWIM	Do what I mean
DWIMC	Do what I mean, correctly
DWISNWID	Do what I say, not what I do
DYJHIW	Don't you just hate it when...
DYK	Do you know

E

EAK	Eating at keyboard
EIE	Enough is enough
EG	Evil grin
EMFBI	Excuse me for butting in
EMFJI	Excuse me for jumping in
EMSG	Email message
EOD	End of discussion
EOF	End of file
EOL	End of lecture
EOM	End of message
EOS	End of story
EOT	End of thread
ETLA	Extended three letter acronym
EYC	Excitable, yet calm

F

F	Female
F/F	Face to face
F2F	Face to face
F2P	Free to play
FAQ	Frequently asked questions
FAWC	For anyone who cares
FBOW	For better or worse
FBTW	Fine, be that way
FCFS	First come, first served

FCOL	For crying out loud
FIFO	First in, first out
FISH	First in, still here
FLA	Four-letter acronym
FOAF	Friend of a friend
FOC	Free of charge
FOCL	Falling of chair laughing
FOFL	Falling on the floor laughing
FOS	Freedom of speech
FOTCL	Falling of the chair laughing
FTF	Face to face
FTTT	From time to time
FUDFUCT	Fear, uncertainty and doubt
FUCT	Failed under continuous testing
FURTB	Full up ready to burst (about hard disk drives)
FW	Freeware
FWIW	For what it's worth
FYA	For your amusement
FYEO	For your eyes only
FYE	For your entertainment
FYEO	For your eyes only
FYI	For your information

G

G	Grin

G2B	Going to bed
G&BIT	Grin & bear it
G2G	Got to go
G2GGS2D	Got to go get something to drink
GA	Go ahead
GA	Good afternoon
GAFIA	Get away from it all
GAL	Get a life
GAS	Greetings and salutations
GBH	Great big hug
GBH&K	Great big hug and kisses
GBR	Garbled beyond recovery
GBY	god bless you
GD&H	Grinning, ducking and hiding
GD&R	Grinning, ducking and running
GD&RAFAP	Grinning, ducking and running as fast as possible
GD&REF&F	Grinning, ducking and running even further and faster
GD&RF	Grinning, ducking and running fast
GD&RVF	Grinning, ducking and running very fast
GD&W	Grin, duck and wave
GDW	Grin, duck and wave
GE	Good evening

GF	Girlfriend
GFETE	Grinning from ear to ear
GFN	Gone for now
GFU	Good for you
GG	Good game
GGU2	Good game you too
GIGO	Garbage in garbage out
GJ	Good job
GL	Good luck
GL&GH	Good luck and good hunting
GM	Good morning / good move / good match
GMAB	Give me a break
GNBLFY	Got nothing but love for you
GMTA	Great minds think alike
GN (GN8)	Good night
GOK	God only knows
GOWI	Get on with it
GPF	General protection fault
GR8	great
GR&D	Grinning, running and ducking
GtG	Got to go
GTSY	Glad to see you

H

H	Hug

H8	Hate (H1 - H9 indicating levels of hate)
H/O	Hold on
H&K	Hug and kiss
HAK	Hug and kiss
HAGD	Have a good day
HAGN	Have a good night
HAGS	Hhave a good summer
HAG1	Have a good one
HAHA	Having a heart attack
HAND	Have a nice day
HB	Hug back
HB	Hurry back
HDYWTDT	How do you work this darn thing
HF	Have fun
HH	Holding hands
HHIS	Hanging head in shame
HHJK	Ha ha, just kidding
HHOJ	Ha ha, only joking
HHOK	Ha ha, only kidding
HHOS	Ha ha, only seriously
HIH	Hope it helps
HILIACACLO	Help I lapsed into a coma and can't log off
HIWTH	Hate it when that happens
HLM	He loves me
HMS	Home made smiley

HMS	hanging myself
HMT	here's my try
HMWK	homework
HOAS	hold on a second
HSIK	how should I know?
HT	heard through
HTH	hope this helps
HTHBE	hope this has been enlightening
HYLMS	hate you like my sister

I

IAAA	I am an accountant
IAAL	I am a lawyer
IAC	in any case
IC	I see
IAE	in any event
IAG	it's all good
IAG	I am gay
IANAA	I am not an accountant
IANAL	I am not a lawyer
INAL	I'm not a lawyer
ICOCBW	I could of course be wrong
IDC	I don't care
IDGI	I don't get it
IDGW	in a good way
IDI	I doubt it
IDK	I don't know
IDTT	I'll drink to that

IFVB	I feel very bad
IGTP	I get the point
IHTFP	I have truly found paradise
IHU	I hate you
IHY	I hate you
II	I'm impressed
IIT	I'm impressed too
IIR	if I recall
IIRC	if I recall correctly
IJWTK	I just want to know
IJWTS	I just want to say
IK	I know
IKWUM	I know what you mean
ILBCNU	I'll be seeing you
ILU	I love you
ILY	I love you
ILYFAE	I love you forever and ever
IMAO	In my arrogant opinion
IMBO	In my bloody opinion
IMCO	In my considered opinion
IME	In my experience
IMHO	In my humble opinion
IMNSHO	In my, not so humble opinion
IMO	In my opinion
IMOBO	In my own biased opinion
IMPOV	In my point of view

IMP	I might be pregnant
INPO	In no particular order
IOW	In other words
IRL	In real life
IRMFI	I reply merely for information
IS	I'm sorry
ISTM	It seems to me
ISTR	I seem to recall
ISWYM	I see what you mean
ITFA	In the final analysis
ITRO	In the reality of
ITRW	In the real world
ITSFWI	If the shoe fits, wear it
IVL	In virtual live
IWALY	I will always love you
IWBNI	It would be nice if
IYKWIM	If you know what I mean
IYSWIM	If you see what I mean

J

JAM	Just a minute
JAS	Just a second
JASE	Just another system error
JAWS	Just another windows shell
JIC	Just in case
JJWY	Just joking with you

JK	Just kidding
J/K	Just kidding
JMHO	Just my humble opinion
JMO	Just my opinion
JP	Just playing
J/P	Just playing
JTLYK	Just to let you know
JW	Just wondering

K

K	OK
K	Kiss
KHYF	Know how you feel
KB	Kiss back
KISS	Keep it simple sister
KIS(S)	Keep it simple (stupid)
KISS	Keeping it sweetly simple
KIT	Keep in touch
KOTC	Kiss on the cheek
KOTL	Kiss on the lips
KPC	Keeping parents clueless
KUTGW	Keep up the good work
KWIM	Know what I mean?

L

L	Laugh
L33t	Elite
L8R	Later
L8R G8R	Later gator

LAM	Leave a message
LBR	Little boys room
LD	Long distance
LG	Lovely greetings
LGR	Little girls room
LHM	Lord help me
LHU	Lord help us
LL&P	Live long & prosper
LNK	Love and kisses
LMA	Leave me alone
LYLAS	Love you like a sister
LULAS	Love you like a sister
LMHO	Laughing my head off
LMIRL	Let's meet in real life
LMK	Let me know
LOL	Laughing out loud
LOL	Lots of love
LOL	Lots of luck
LOLA	Laughing out loud again
LOML	Light of my life (or love of my life)
LOMLILY	Light of my life, I love you
LOOL	Laughing out outrageously loud
LSHMBB	Laughing so hard my belly is bouncing
LSHMBH	Laughing so hard my belly hurts
LTNS	Long time no see
LTR	Long term relationship

LTS	Laughing to self
LUWAMH	Love you with all my heart
LY	Love ya
LYK	Let you know
LYL	Love ya lots
LYLAB	Love ya like a brother
LYLAS	Love ya like a sister

M

M	Male
MB	Maybe
MYOB	Mind your own business
MWBRL	More Will Be Revealed Later
M8	Mate

N

N	In
N2M	Not too much
N/C	Not cool
NALOPKT	Not a lot of people know that
NE1	Anyone
NETUA	Nobody ever tells us anything
N1	Nice one
NL	Not likely
NM	Never mind / nothing much

N/M	Never mind / nothing much
NMH	Not much here
NMJC	Nothing much, just chillin'
NOM	No offence meant
NOTTOMH	Not of the top of my mind
NOYB	none of your business
NP	No problem
NTA	Non-technical acronym
NVM	Nevermind

O

OBTW	Oh, by the way
OIC	Oh, I see
OF	On fire
OFIS	On floor with stitches
OH	Overheard
OK	Abbreviation of oll korrect (all correct)
OL	Old lady (wife, girlfriend)
OLL	On-line love
OM	Old man (husband, boyfriend)
OMG	Oh my god / gosh / goodness
OOC	Out of character
OT	Off topic / other topic
OTOH	On the other hand

OTP	On the phone
OTTOMH	Off the top of my head

P

PAW	Parents are watching
PDS	Please don't shoot
PEBCAK	Problem exists between chair and keyboard
PLZ	Please
PM	Private message
PMJI	Pardon my jumping in (Another way for PMFJI)
PMFJI	Pardon me for jumping in
POAHF	Put on a happy face
POOF	I have left the chat
POTB	Pats on the back
POS	Parents over shoulder
POTS	Parents over the shoulder - (My parents are watching, I can't really talk)
PPL	People
PS	Post script
PSA	Public show of affection
P911	Parent emergency

Q

Q4U	Question for you

QSL	Reply
QSO	Conversation
QT	Cutie

R

RAT	Remote(ly) activated Trojan
RCed	Reconnected
RE	Hi again (same as re's)
ROFL	Rolling on floor laughing
ROFLOLAY	Rolling on floor laughing out loud at you
ROFLOLTSDMC	Rolling on floor laughing out loud tears streaming down my cheeks
ROFLOLWTIME	Rolling on floor laughing out loud with tears in my eyes
ROFLOLUTS	Rolling on floor laughing out loud unable to speak
ROTFL	Rolling on the floor laughing
RT	ReTweet (Repeat or forwarding for Twitters instead of emails)
RM	Remake
RTF	Read the FAQ
RTM	Read the manual
RTSM	Read the stupid manual

RUMOF	Are you male or female?
RUTTM	Are you talking to me?
RUUP4IT	Are you up for it?
RVD	Really very dumb

S

S2R	Send to receive
SAMAGAL	Stop annoying me and get a life
SCNR	Sorry, could not resist
SETE	Smiling ear to ear
SGTM	Silently giggling to myself
SH	So hot
SH	Same here
SHID	Slaps head in disgust
SHMILY	See how much I love you
SIF	As if
SO	Significant other
SOHF	Sense of humour failure
SOMY	Sick of me yet?
SPAM	Stupid persons' advertisement
SRY	Sorry
STBY	Sucks to be you
STW	Search the web
SWAK	Sealed with a kiss
SWALK	Sweet, with all love, kisses
SWL	Screaming with laughter

SIM	Sh*t, it's Monday
SITWB	Sorry, in the wrong box
S/U	Shut up
SYS	See you soon
SYSOP	System operator

T

TA	Thanks again
TAW	Teachers are watching
TCO	Taken care of
TGIF	Thank god its Friday
THTH	Too hot to handle
THX	Thanks
TIA	Thanks in advance
TIIC	The idiots in charge
TJM	That's just me
TLA	Three-letter acronym
TMA	Take my advice
TMI	Too much information
TMS	Too much showing
TNSTAAFL	There's no such thing as a free lunch
TNX	Thanks
TOH	To other half
TOY	Thinking of you
TPTB	The powers that be
TSDMC	Tears streaming down my cheeks

TT2T	Too tired to talk
TTFN	Ta ta for now
TTT	Thought that, too
TTYIAM	Talk to you in a minute
TTYL	Talk to you later
TTYLMF	Talk to you later my friend
TTYS	Talk to you soon
TU	Thank you
TWMA	Till we meet again
TX	Thanks
TY	Thank you
TYVM	Thank you very much

U

U2	You too
UR	Your
UW	You're welcome
URAQT!	You are a cutie!

V

VBG	Very big grin
VBS	Very big smile

W

W8	Wait
W8AM	Wait a minute

WAY	What about you?
WAY	Who are you?
WB	Welcome back
WBS	Write back soon
WDHLM	Why doesn't he love me?
WDYWTTA	What Do You Want To Talk About
WE	Whatever
W/E	Whatever
WFM	Works for me
WNDITWB	We never did it this way before
WP	Wrong person
WRT	With respect to
WTG	Way to go
WTGP	Want to go private?
WTH	What/who the heck?
WTMI	Way to much information
WU	What's up?
WU@	What/where you at?
WUF	Where are you from?
WUU2	What you up to?
WUWT	What's up with that?
WYCM?	Will you call me?
WYMM	Will you marry me?
WYRN	What's Your Real Name?
WYSIWYG	What you see is what you get

X

XTLA	Extended three letter acronym

Y

Y	Why?
Y2K	You're too kind
YATB	You are the best
YBS	You'll be sorry
YG	Young gentleman
YKYWTKM	You know you want to kiss me
YL	Young lady
YL	You 'll live
YM	You mean
YM	Young man
YMMD	You've made my day
YMMV	Your mileage may vary
YVM	You're very welcome
YW	You're welcome
YWIA	You're welcome in advance
YWTHM	You want to hug me
YWTLM	You want to love me
YWTKM	You want to kiss me
YOYO	You're on your own
YY4U	Too wise for you

Z

ZZZ	Sleeping, bored, tired

More...........

?	Huh?
?4U	Question for you
143	I Love You
2U2	To you too
2MFM	To much for me
420 4life	Marijuana
4AYN	For all you know
4ever	Forever
4COL	For crying out loud
4SALE	For sale
4U	For you
=w=	Whatever
G	Giggle or grin
H	Hug
K	Kiss
S	Smile
T	Tickle
W	Wink

MORE CHAT ROOM SLANG

Chat Slang Dictionary = most frequently used in PULPchat

*	Your actions in the third person, i.e. " *goes to your site"
<3	Love, i.e. "I <3 New York" (looks like a sideways heart)
</3	Broken Heart / Hearted, i.e. "She left me and I'm </3"
adn	Any Day Now
afk	Away From Keyboard
afn	That's All For Now
asap	As Soon As Possible
asl?, a/s/l	What's your Age, Sex, and Location?
atm	At The Moment
b4	Before
bbl	Be Back Later
bc, b/c	Because
bf	Boyfriend
bfn	Bye For Now
brb	Be Right Back
btdt	Been There, Done That
btw	By The Way
cu	See You
cya	See Ya

d/w	Don't Worry
dl, d/l	Download, Downloading; ALSO "down low"
eg	Evil Grin
emsg	Email Message
f2f	Face To Face
fyi	For Your Information
gal	Get A Life
gf	Girlfriend
gg, g/g	Gotta Go
gl	Good Luck
gmta	Great Minds Think Alike
gr	Gotta Run
gtg, g2g	Got To Go, Gotta Go
gtsy	Glad To See You
h&k	A Hug and a Kiss
h/o	Hold On
hb	Hurry Back
hw	Homework
ianal	I Am Not A Lawyer but...
idk	I Don't Know
im	Instant Message
imho	In My Humble Opinion
imo	In My Opinion
irl	In Real Life
jk, j/k	Just Kidding
jtlyk	Just To Let You Know
jw	Just Wondering
k, kk	Okay, alright

kit	Keep In Touch
kthx	Okay Thanks
kthxbi	Okay Thanks, Bye
l8r	Later (Goodbye)
lol	Laughing Out Loud
ltns	Long Time No See
lyl	Love Ya Lots!
lylab	Love Ya Like A Brother
lylas	Love Ya Like A Sister
mwa	A Kiss (the sound "mwa")
nc, n/c	No Comment
nm, n/m	Never Mind
np	No Problem
nvm	Never Mind
oic	Oh, I See
ol	Old Lady (wife, girlfriend)
om	Old Man (husband, boyfriend)
omg!	Oh My Gosh!, Oh My God!
otp	On The Phone
pal	Parents Are Listening
pls, plz	Please
pm	Private Message
pmfji	Pardon Me For Jumping In
pos	Parent Over Shoulder
ppl	People, i.e. "lotsa ppl do that"

qt	Cutie
r	Are, i.e. "what r u doing?"
rl	Real Life
rofl	Rolling On Floor Laughing
sb	Smiles Back
so	Significant Other
srsly	Seriously
sry	Sorry
sup?	What's up? or Wassup? (a greeting)
sys	See You Soon
ta	Thanks Again
thx	Thanks
ttfn	Ta Ta For Now
ttyl	Talk To You Later
ty	Thank You
tyt	Take Your Time (common reply to brb)
u	You
ul, u/l	Upload or Uploading
ur	Your
vn	Very Nice
w.e	Whatever
w/e	Whatever
wb	Welcome Back
weg	Wicked Evil Grin
wtgp?	Want To Go Private? (go to a private room)

wth?	What The Heck? or What The Hell?
xoxo	Hugs and Kisses (X's are kisses and O's are hugs)
ybs	You'll Be Sorry
yt?	You There?
yw	Your Welcome

VOCABULARY
Single letters can replace words

be becomes *b*
see becomes *c*
okay becomes *k*
okay cool becomes *kk*
are becomes *r*
you becomes *u*
why becomes *y*
oh becomes *o*

Single Digits Can Replace Words

ate becomes *8*
for becomes *4*
to or *too* becomes *2*
won or *one* becomes *1*

A Single Letter or Digit Can Replace A Syllable

ate becomes *8*, so:

great becomes gr8
mate becomes m8
wait becomes w8
later becomes l8r or l8a
skate becomes sk8
skater becomes sk8r

tomorrow becomes *2mro*

for or *fore* becomes *4*, so:

before becomes (combining both of the above) b4
therefore becomes thr4

once becomes *1ce*

and becomes *&*, *nd*

Combinations of The Above Can Shorten A Single Or Multiple Words

Your and ***You're*** become ***ur***, ***yr***, or ***u're***

EMOTICONS

An emoticon is a facial expression pictorially represented by punctuation and letters, usually to express a writer's mood.

Emoticons are often used to alert a responder to the tenor or temper of a statement, and can change and improve the interpretation of plain text.

The word is a *portmanteau* of the *English* words *emotion* (or *emote*) and *icon*.

The use of emoticons can be traced back to the 19th century, and they were commonly used in casual and/or humorous writing.

Digital forms of emoticons on the *Internet* were included in a proposal by *Scott Fahlman* of *Carnegie Mellon University* in a message on 19 September 1982.

ORIGINAL SMILEY FACES

:)	Original smiley
:-)	Classic smiley
;-)	Wink
:-))	Very happy
|-)	Hee-hee
:-D	Laugh loud
:-o	Amazement
:^D"	Great! I like it!
:-*	Kiss
<3	I love you
:-s	Confusion
{}	No comment
:-C	Totally unbelievable
:-X	Big wet kiss
:-9	Licking lips
%-)	Confused
:	Fuzzy face
:-@	Screaming
:-7	Wry remark
:-p	Sticking out tongue
:-(	Frown
:>	Devilish grin
(:-|K-	Dressed to kill

:-||	Angry
::=))	Seeing double
:->	Hey
|:-0	No explanation
#:-)	Hair in a mess
>;-('	I am spitting mad
#-)	Partied all night
:-|	Hmmm
:-&	Tongue-tied
~#:-(	Bad hair day
:'-(	I am crying
:*)	I' tipsy
:-o	Oh
O:-)	Innocent
&:-)	Sender has curly hair
(:-...	Heart-broken
%-)	Tipsy but happy
#:-o	Oh no!
:-#	My lips are sealed
8-)	Sender wears glasses
:+(	I'm hurt by that
:*)?	Are you drunk?
<:-0	Eeek!
:-e	I'm disappointed
(-:	Sender is left-handed
<:-)	Dumb question
~o~	Bird
:@	Ouch!
:-(*)	Sick comment

(:-)	Bald
://	Frustrated
:3-<	Dog
d:-)	Hats off to your great idea
:-$	Put your money where your mouth is
:-{)	Sender has moustache
|-|	Going to sleep
:@)	Pig
\o/	Praise the Lord
*<:o)	Clown
:-{)}	Sender has moustache and beard
:=8)	Baboon
8^	Chicken

NUMERIC SMS

:-0 hbtu 0-:	Happy birthday to you
@WRK	At work
2bctnd	To be continued.
2d4	To die for
2g4u	To good for you
2Ht2Hndl	Too hot to handle.
2l8	Too late
2WIMC	To whom it may concern
4e	Forever
4yeo	For your eyes only

MORE .....

KNOWLEDGE
Knowledge is the color black, the way the color black never ends.

BITE OF U
The length & breadth & height of you
total up to quite a view,
but to taste the true delight of you
I'll have to take a bite of you.

UR SMILE
Your smile is a general
my heart a soldier

STARS
If the universe did start with a bang
when God loved and the angels sang
one of the sparks that flew
chased time to become you

KISS
If kisses wer rain id send u showers,
if fun was time id send u hrs,
if u needed a frnd id send u me!

BOOK OF LIFE
Starting a new day,
Starting a new life,
Starting a new page,
In the Endless Book of Life.

LETTING GO
if i luv sum1 let them go...
if they return it was meant to b...
if they dont their luv was never yours 2 begin with

Forget Me Not

forgettin you is hard to do
forgettin me is up to you
forget me not
forget me never
forget this message
but not the sender

Sent With A Smile

god in heaven,
god above
please protect the one i love,
sent with a smile,
sealed with a kiss,
i love the one who is reading this

Stolen

Your words of love steal
someone's heart,
but you don't know that your
heart is already stolen by me,
check it!

Found You

I love you up from heaven
down to the ground
I'm really glad
to have you found

Dont4get

Please remind me 2 remind u about reminding me 2 send u this reminder that reminds me of reminding u that i am always ur friend. DONT 4GET!

How Much U Mean 2 Me

If i go 2 heaven an ur not der i'll write ur name on evry stair 4 all 2 c how much u mean 2 me

Too Much!

when God gave us friendships he tried to be fair, but when i got you, i got more than my share!

Fall

U can fall from the sky
U can fall from a tree
But the best way to fall
is in love with me.

4ever

u r me, and i is u for eva our love will be true

Meant 2 B

i love u babe i really do, i love the times when im with u, the way u say that u love me, i think that this was meant to be

Stolen

Your words of love steal
someone's heart,
but you don't know that your
heart is already stolen by me,
check it!

Ma Huni

Gifts r given @ b'days, chocs @ valentine, roses 2 say sorry, luv is shown wid kisses, but da reason 4 sending dis is.... cuz UR MA HUNI!!

Coz

It must have been a rainy day! when u were born heaven was crying coz it lost it's most beautiful angel...

Among The Stars

Among the stars you´re the one that shines the most. Among the winds you´re the one that brings the warm air. Among the people you´re the one who I wanna give a rose.

I Miss U

I miss u wen ur far away,i think bout u evry nite n day i really cant believe its true dat 1 day ill b bak wth u.

Falling

You can fall from the sky.
You can fall from a tree but you will get hurt.
But falling in love with me is like falling in heaven!

Evry Nite

Every night when I look at the moon, it reminds me of you, how you can see the same moon. It makes me sometimes sad because I can see the moon, but I can´t see you.

Learn 2 Luv

Learn 2 love the people who are willing to love U at present.4get the people in the past & tnk dem 4 hurting U which led U 2 luv d people U have right now

LOVE SMS

The one thing we can never get enough of is love. And the one thing we never give enough is love. Henry Miller

- **Love** many things, for therein lies the true strength, and whosoever loves much performs much, and can accomplish much, and what is done in love is done well. -Vincent van Gogh

- **Love** is the emblem of eternity; it confounds all notions of time; effaces all memory of beginning, all fear of an end. -Madame de Stael

- **If** you truly love someone, then the only thing you want for them is to be happy....even if its not with you. -Lauren&L

- **I** have no regrets. I will never regret loving someone because the feeling of love for five minutes is greater than an eternity of hurt. -Kurt Langner

- **Expect** the people you love to be better. It helps them to become better. But don't get upset when they fail. It helps them keep trying. –Anonymous

- **The** beginning of love is to let those we love be perfectly themselves, and not to twist them to fit our own image. Otherwise we love only the reflection of ourselves we find in them. -Thomas Merton

- **When** you feel cold and warm at the same time, when you read over the same line for the tenth time, when your heart and thoughts somehow appear to rhyme, and when a simple name conquers your whole mind, then you are in deep trouble my friend... you are in what they call, "love". -Philippos Aristotelous

Many a man in love with a dimple makes the mistake of marrying the whole girl. -Stephen B. Leacock

You can't buy love, but you can pay heavily for it. -Henny Youngman

"**A** bell's not a bell 'til you ring it A song's not a song 'til you sing it Love in your heart wasn't put there to stay Love isn't love 'til you give it away!" -Oscar Hammerstein

Love is giving someone the ability to destroy you and trusting them not to.

Pure love and suspicion cannot dwell together: at the door where the latter enters, the former makes its exit.-Alexander Dumas

Doubt that the stars are fire, doubt that the sun doth move, doubt truth to be a liar, but never doubt I love. -William Shakespeare

Men love because they are afraid of themselves, afraid of the loneliness that lives in them, and need someone in whom they can lose themselves as smoke loses itself in the sky. -V.F. Calverton

Absence is to love as wind is to fire; it extinguishes the small and kindles the great. -Roger de Bussy-Rabutin

Trouble is a part of your life, and if you don't share it, you don't give the person who loves you a chance to love you enough. -Dinah Shore

Love is missing someone whenever you're apart, but somehow feeling warm inside because you're close in heart. -Kay Knudsen

Love has nothing to do with what you are expecting to get, it's what you are expected to give -- which is everything.

Just because somebody doesn't love you the way you want them to, doesn't mean they don't love you with all they have.

You don't love a woman because she is beautiful, she is beautiful because you love her.

You come to love not by finding the perfect person, but by seeing an imperfect person perfectly. -Sam Keen

Immature love says, 'I love you because I need you.' Mature love says, 'I need you because I love you.' -Erich Fromm

If you have love in your life it can make up for a great many things you lack. If you don't have it, no matter what else there is, it's not enough. -Ann Landers

Love at first sight is easy to understand; it's when two people have been looking at each other for a lifetime that it becomes a miracle. -Amy Bloom

The Grand essentials of happiness are: something to do, something to love, and something to hope for. -Allan K. Chalmers

THE LIGHTER VEIN

Marriage is a 3-ring circus - engagement ring, wedding ring and suffering.

It's better to let someone think you are an Idiot than to open your mouth and prove it.

Marriage is not a word. It's a sentence....(a life sentence!).

A good friend is like a computer; me 'enter' ur life, 'save' u in my heart, 'format' ur problems, 'shift' u 2 opportunities & never 'delete' u from my memory!

If someone comes into your life and becomes part of you, but for some reason he/she could not stay, don't be too sad... be glad that your paths have crossed

Dont have an attitude problem. You have a perception problem!

A hangover is the wrath of grapes

Out of my mind. Back in five minutes

"Please, Lord, let me prove that winning the lottery won't spoil me."

"Yes, this is my pickup. No, I will not help you move."

"We will now upgrade your brain, please wait... searching...searching.....more

Some things are left undone, some words are left unsaid, some feelings are left unexpressed, but someone as sweet as you could never be left unmissed.

Principles of student life. Love your bed, It's your temple. Relax in the days, so that you can sleep at night. Books are holy, so don't touch

I have a heart n that is true, But now it has gone from me to you, So care for it just like I do, Because I have no heart n U have two.

Friendship is not about finding similarities, it is about respecting differences. You are not my friend coz you are like me, but because i accept you and respect you the way you are.

The worst way to miss someone is to be sitting right beside them knowing you can't have them.

Some things are left undone, some words are left unsaid, some feelings are left unexpressed, but someone as sweet as you could never be left unmissed.

Principles of student life.Love your bed, Its your temple. Relax in the days, so that you can sleep at night. Books are holy, so don't touch

I have a heart n that is true, But now it has gone from me to you,So care for it just like I do, Because I have no heart n U have two.

Friendship is not about finding similarities, it is about respecting differences. You are not my friend coz you are like me, but because i accept you and respect you the way you are.

The worst way to miss someone is to be sitting right beside them knowing you can't have them.

I am in hospital now. After 5 minutes, I will be transferred to a surgery room. The doctor told me, I will die if I stop RECEIVING YOUR SMS.

If you fall into river there is a boat .. if you fall in a well there is a rope .. but if you fall in love there is no hope

If U delete this message thats bcoz u love me. ... If u save it thats bcoz u desire me .. & if u ignore it thats bcoz u miss me. So what u gonna do with It?

Do you believe in love at first sight .. or do I have to walk by again??

Love is sweet poison: .. Do not consume without your beloveds advise .. and keep out of reach of children .. and keep it in cool and dark place.

If you love someone, put their name in a circle, instead of a heart, because hearts can break, but circles go on forever

You are like the sunshine so warm, you are like sugar, so sweet... you are like you... and that's the reason why I love you!

You must be a good runner because you are always running in my mind, you must be a good thief because you have stolen my heart, and i am always a bad shooter because I Miss You Always...

I have the "I",I have the "L",I have the "O",I have the "V",I have the

"**E**",... so pls can I have "U"?

What I feel for you, is really true. You got to know,I need you so. When you are gone,I cant go on. Can't you see, that you are the only one for me?

Love is like a golden chain that links our hearts together and if you ever break that chain you'll break my heart 4ever!

Sweet as a rose bud bright as a star cute as a kitten thats what u are.bundles of joy sunshine and fun you are everything i luv all rolled into 1

I have liked many but loved very few. yet no-one has been as sweet as u. Id stand and wait in the worlds longest queue.just for the pleasure of a moment with u.

Sometimes My eyes get jealous of my Heart!!!

You Know Why?Bcoz.....You Always Remain close to my HEART n far from my EYES.

uv been called b4 cupids court 4 stealin my heart.trespassin in my dreams & robin me of my senses.uv been sentened 2 a lifetime wiv me- how do u plead?

I love so much my heart is sure.As time goes on I love you more,Your happy smile.Your loving face, no one will ever take your place

Ur only mine wen i dream.wen i wake i wanna scream.ur not mine im all alone.i can only text u on my fone.do dreams lie or r dey true-i hope so cos babes i want u!

I believe that God above created u for me to luv. he picked you out from all the rest cos he knew id luv you the best!

Today a few drops of blood fell down of my heart and when i asked why the response was "There was someone very cruel in yours heart that forced us to come out.

Love is just like life, it's not always easy and does not always bring happiness. but when we do not stop living why should we stop loving

Remember me like pressed flower in ur Notebook. It may not b having any fragrance,but will remind u of my existence 4ever in ur life...

My love that shall not die, till the sun grows cold, and the stars grow old

Love is like swallowing hot chocolate, it takes you by surprise at first, but keeps you warm for a long time

My love for you is a journey, starting at forever and ending at never

I m feeling so happy, do u know why? cuz i m so lucky, do u know how? cuz God loves me.Do u know how? cuz he gave me a gift. Do u know what? its YOU my love.

Have a cigar daily - U'ill die 10 yrs early.

Have drinks daily - U'll die 30 yrs early.

Luv someone truly - U'll die daily.

When time comes for u to give ur heart to someone, make sure u select someone who will never break ur heart, cuz broken hearts has never spare parts.

Love that we cannot have is the one that lasts the longest, hurts the deepest and feels the strongest.

I love all the stars in the sky, but they are nothing compared to the ones in your eyes

I finally got my past, present and future tenses correct today. I loved you. I love you. I will love you forever.

Everyone says you only fall in love once but that's wrong, everytime I see your smile I fall in love all over again. Luv You!

If you love someone, put their name in a circle, instead of a heart, because hearts can break, but circles go on forever.

What I feel for you,is really true. You got to know,I need you so. When you are gone,I can't go on. Can't you see, that you are the only one for me?

FLIRT SMS

1+1=2 eyes look at u...
12+12=24 hours thinking about u...
3+4=7 days in week missing u...
   1+11=12 months I always need A SWEET PERSON like U.

The moment I first saw you, you warmed my heart, the second time you made little flames and now you make my heart burn like hearth !

What is the difference between your and my smile?
U smile when you are happy
and I smile when you are happy.

Never get tired of doing little things to others,
coz sumtimes those little things may mean so much to them.
That is why I wont get tired of sending my little Hi to U.

I cant help it, its not by choice,
my heart beats faster, my knees get weak,
my stomach hurts & I can hardly breathe and each & every moment feels brand new,
I just cant help it I am crazy for U!

U luk sweet when u read my message.
U luk sweeter when u read my message & smile.
U luk sweetest when u read my message, smile & reply. So, try to look sweetest.

Government imposing new taxes.
Dating ₹ 10, Hug ₹ 200, Kiss ₹ 300, Love ₹ 500.
But you dont worry, flirting is still free.

New style of proposing a girl..
"i hv spent many sleepless nights
in ur Luv n i dont want my son 2 do d same
4 your daughter so lets mk them brother n sister

Do u know whats A B C D E F G?
A Boy Can Do Everything For Girl
Now reverse da order, can u guess the full form of: G F E D C B A?
Girls Forgets Everything Done & Catches (new) Boy Again.

I heard that good looks can kill...
So, please don't look at me
I don't wanna see you die.!!!

Life is pretty much unpredictable. I may not live long enough but I won't miss out letting you know that life is worth living with someone like you around.

Having a good laugh with a friend like you stimulates endorphins, the brain's natural painkillers. So, if you need to laugh and you can't find a friend like yourself, I can lend you my mirror.

A smile is the best lighting system of the face, the best cooling system of the head, and the best warming system of the heart. Keep smiling!

It takes a strong heart to love. It takes a stronger heart to continue to love after it has been hurt...
Always be Happy, always wear a smile;
Not because life is full of reasons to smile but because ur smile itself is a reason for many others to smile...

One who smokes, has a SMOKY heart,
One who drinks, has an ALCOHOLIC heart...
So dear U must STOP eating SWEETS...
as u r already a SWEET HEART!

If I could be any part of you, I'd be your tear. To be conceived in your heart, born in your eyes, live on your cheeks, and die on your lips.

Love bears all things,
Love believes all things,
Love hopes all things,
and most precious of all,
Love endures all things.
Come we love and make things happy.

What is the height of Flirting?
When your love letter starts with
"TO WHOMSOEVER IT MAY CONCERN".

I think you are very careless! U come & leave things behind! See now what u have left? U just came in my mind and left a smile on my face.

I believe that God above created you for me to luv. He picked me out from all the rest coz he knew I'd luv you the best!

U luk sweet when u read my message. U luk sweeter when u read my message & smile. U luk sweetest when u read my message, smile & reply. So, try to look sweetest.

As days go by, my feelings get stronger,
To be in ur arms, I can't wait any longer.
Look into my eyes & u'll see that it's true,
Day & night my thoughts r of U.

I wish I was a teddy bear, that lay upon your bed, so everytime you cuddled it, you cuddled me instead.

Even if I had 1 wish... I wouldn't wish for u to love me, coz I don't want your love to come from a wish... but straight from your heart.

My heart problem has
reached a critical stage.
That doctor says:
There r only 2 options left...
ICU
Or
U C Me.

Be careful
when
a gal tells u that
she loves u
from the bottom of her heart.
For this may mean
that there is
still enough space
for another boy
on top!

I always think about U.
I cant live without U.
I really need U.
I am totally mad about U.
I just wanna be with U.
I am crazy 4 U.
I wanna marry U.
I LOVE U.
U = Ur friend

Those who can't have u hate u, those who have u can't handle u, those who abuse u lose u, & then there are those like me who just can't refuse u!

Too many stars in the sky, too many tears that have left my eyes. Too many girls out in the blue, but they are nothing compared to you!

Sharp is ur memory, sweet is ur name, deep in my heart u'll always remain. Earth wants water, flower wants dew, I want nothing but a smile from u.

U may b out of my sight but not out of my heart. U may b out of my reach but not out of my mind. I don't know what I mean 2 u, but u'll always be special 2 me.

All I wanted was sumone 2 care 4 me. All I wanted was sumone who'd b there 4 me. All I ever wanted was sumone who'd b true. All I ever wanted was sum1 like u.

Touch my heart & u'll feel,
Listen to my heart & u'll hear,
Look into my heart & u'll see,
That u'll always be a special part of me.

Don't send any messages, I don't want to see you, hear your voice, think of you, coz my doctor advised me 2 keep away from Sweets.

If u see some one without a smile, give him one of urns, coz u r among a few good people who can shine others lives by just walking with him a few miles.

I know you think I'm cute, I know you think I'm fine, but like the other guys, take a number and wait in line!

Hello!! What's wrong with your mobile?
Tried so many times but Every time I call it says: The subscriber you are trying to reach is in your heart!

In da mornin I don't eat coz I think of u, at noon I don't eat coz I think of u, in da evenin I don't eat coz I think of u, at night I don't sleep coz Im hungry

---

If all the girls lived on the other side of the sea, what a good swimmer I would be?

Excuse me, do u have a Band-Aid? I skinned my knee when I fell for you.

Without ur SMS days are like: Moanday, Tearsday, Wasteday, Thirstday, Frightday, Shattereday & Sadday. So send me SMS everyday.

U may be out of my sight, but not out of my heart. U may be out of my reach, but not out of my mind. I may mean nothing to u but u'll always be special to me.

Hey, I just got your blood test report. U have been tested HIV positive. Report reads person has high percentage of Honey In Veins. No Wonder!

Only the open heart receives love, only the open mind receives wisdom, only the open hand receives gifts and only the cute persons receive SMS from me!

A mobile is like women - Talks non-stop, costs a fortune, disturbs when u r busy and when u need them urgently they have no service.

I want u ... To be with me In a nice Rastaurent To have candle light dinner.... & to say those sweet three words to U.... "Pay The Bill"

I used to think that dreams do not come true, but this quickly changed the moment I laid my eyes on you.

Faith makes all things possible, love makes all things easy, hopes makes all things work, but ur gorgeous smile brings all faith, luv & hope in me!

Little keys can open big locks, simple words can express great thoughts. A text from u never fails to make me smile the whole day through.

If you say my eyes are beautiful it's because they're looking at you, for my eyes are just the windows my feelings come through.

Walk with me when ur hearts needs company, take my hand when u feel all alone, turn to me when u need some1 to lean on, coz I'm the one u can always depend on!

A - U'r Attractive
B - U'r D Best
C - U'r Cute
D - U'r Dear 2 me
E - U'r Excellent
F - U'r Funny
G - U'r Gud Looking
H - He He He
I - I'm
J - Just
K - Kidding

MISS YOU SMS

There's no Special reason for this msg, I juz wanna steal a single moment out of ur busy life & hope I can make u smile n say: I Miss U.

Do u know, what I say, what I think, what I feel, what I think, what I wish, U want to know? I MISS U SO MUCH.

U must b tired coz u hv been running through my mind, u gotta b a thief coz u hv stolen my heart n I must hv been a bad shooter coz I keep missing u.

In The Flower My Rose Is You,
In The Diamond My Kohinoor Is You,
In The Sky My Moon Is You,
I'm Only Body My Heart Is You,
That's Why I Always MISS YOU!

Close your Eyes,
Relax your Body,
And stop your Breathing as long as you can...
NOW BREATH......
I Miss you as much as YOU MISSED THE AIR!

Whenever I miss You, Stars falls down from the Sky.
So any day if you find the sky empty, don't blame me!

It's all your fault; You made me Miss You So Much!!

Last night i wanted to send u a msg, but all i could write was: "noh ss!w !". it didn't make much sense until i read it upside down...

If u wanna know how much I miss u,
try to catch rain drops,
the ones u catch is how much u miss me,
and the ones u miss is how much I miss u

I hide my tears when I say your name, but the pain in my heart is still the same. Although I Smile & Seem Carefree, There is no one Who misses you more than ME!

Wat makes some people dearer is not just de happiness dat u feel when u meet them but de pain u feel when u miss them.. MISS U........
Do u know, what i say, what i think, what i feel, what i think, what i wish, U want to know? I MISS U SO MUCH.

A B C D E F G H I J K L M N O P Q R S T " " V W X Y Z.Did i miss something.No,i put 'U' safely in my heart

Earth may stop rotating, birds may stop flying, candles may stop melting,fish may stop swiming,heat may stop beating but i never stop missing u......

If u think i miss u all the time u r wrong i miss u only when i think about u but Damm it i think u all the time i miss u sweetheart.

When you feel lonely press 945, when you feel sad press 10, when u need to talk, press 82,,,when u press all these together, here i m for u always. Miss u alot.

Just Wondering..!
Wud U Smile At Me If I Smile At U..?
Wud U Say Hello If I Greet U..?
Wud U Talk 2 Me If I Talk 2 U..?
Wud U Add "Too" If I Tell U "I Miss U"..?
Really I Miss U From The Core !

To forget is hard to do, and to forget me is upto u, forget me forget me never,forget the text but not the sender.Miss you a lot.

Under the sea, there lies a rock. In the rock, there is an envelope. In the envelope, there is a paper. On the paper, there are 3 words... 'I Miss You'.

There are 24 hours in a DayNight, 10 hours for work, 8 hours for sleeping, 3 hours for eating, 2 hours for exercise and 1 hour for other activities, But all the 24 hours I do MISS U badly...

when i close my eyes before sleeping i watch u in the dark, When im sleeping i watch u in my dreams, When i open my eyes i found u before my eyes..And then I start Missing u for all the Day...

i miss u very much,but i know u miss me not. MISS ME OTHERWISE U WILL MISS ME FOREVER.

Can u keep a secret?
Between me & u
You promise?
I really need to tell u this...
Well...
I MISS U...

In My Lyf..I learned how 2 smile.How 2 Laugh. How 2 HardWork.How 2 Love.How 2 cry..but i neva learned how 2 stop MISSING YOU!

143 is numerically saying "I MISS YOU" What if I ask u 23423 same as "DO YOU MISS ME TOO? Would u answer me 312 same as "YES I DO"

u r in my talks.u r in my eyes.u r in my feelings. u r in my thoughts.u r in my breath.u r in my work.u r in my mind.u r in my dreams.u r in my prayer.u r in my life.because u r in my heart.I miss u.

A simple Bye makes us cry,
A simple Joke makes us laugh,

A simple Care makes us fall in love.
I hope my simple SMS makes you think of me.
I Miss U

The sun refused to shine the day you went away and though i try to smile my heart is ever gray you left a wound inside my heart and now i'm sad and blue plz pick up the phone and call me. I MISS U.

I may seldom tell u how special u are, I may not b able to reach u coz we're both busy, but in spite of all, u know u are someone I really miss & care about.

Always knew that looking back on my tears would someday make me laugh, but I never knew that looking back on my laughter would someday make me cry. Miss you.

Love, i wish i didn't know you in the 1st place.... so that when u're gone, i won't be missing u like this.....gosh,just how i wanted to be with you.... girl, i miss u.

When the weather comes true
I miss u
When the flower covered dew
i miss u
When the day comes new
I miss u

No words i write can ever say
how much i miss you everyday.
as time goes by the loneliness grows,
how i miss you... nobody knows.

Today i miss u
Yesterday i missed u.
Don't worry about tomorrow, i'll always miss u,
and that is a promise. Miss U Forever.

Ever since you ve left i ve
realised that a part of one`s
Life is made of someone
else`s life ,
I MISS THAT PART .
I MISS YOU.

Days r too busy. Hours r too few.
Seconds r too fast.
but ther is alwys a tym,
for me to ask how r u? hope
u r fine.. miss u..

Whenever I miss You, Stars falls down from the Sky.
So any day if you find the sky empty, don't blame me!
It's all your fault; You made me Miss You So Much

There are 2 types of enjoyment. One is being with a friend. The other is being with the memories of friends. Miss u but not ur memories.

Nobody is right till somebody is wrong... Nobody is weak till somebody is strong... Nobody is lucky till love comes along... Nobody is lonely till somebody is gone. Missing U!

Do u know, what I say, what I think, what I feel, what I think, what I wish, U want to know? I MISS U SO MUCH

Relationship is like a Violin, music may stop now & then, but strings are attached forever. So if u b in touch or not, u r always remembered. Miss U!

Press down if you miss me. So U Miss Me
Ok You Can Stop
Still Pressing
Well, I miss you too.

Changes in life are good, but see to that changes don't take you far away from the people who love and care you...including myself. Missing U!

LATEST & NEW SMS

Cell Phone
Causes Radiation
& It Results In
Brain Damage !
But You are Safe.
It Only Affects
People With

Brains !!
How Lucky you are , No Brain No Pain.

Equipped with his five senses,
man explores the universe around him and calls
the adventure Science.

Old wood best to burn.
Old books best to read.
Old rice best to eat
and old friends best to keep.

GIRL before marriage looks like Brbie doll,
After marriage Beautiful doll,
after one year Nice doll,
after two years only doll,
after three years
PANADOL.

Age appears to be best in some things.
Old wood best to burn.
Old books best to read.
Old rice best to eat
and old friends best to keep.

Do Not Go Where The Path May Lead,
Go Instead Where There Is No
Path And Leave A Trail..

Love me but, leave me not,
Kiss me but, miss me not,
Hit me but, hate me not,
Remember me but, forget me not.

For last year's words belong to last year's language
And next year's words await another voice.
And to make an end is to make a beginning.
Happy New Year.

ROMANTIC SMS

Don't wait until it's too late to tell
someone how much you love, how much you care.
Because when they're gone, no matter how loud
you shout and cry, they won't hear you anymore.

All I Wanted Was SomeOne To Care For Me
All I Wanted Was SomeOne Who Would Be There For Me
All I Ever Wanted Was SomeOne Who Would Be True
All I Ever Wanted Was SomeOne like You.

Love isn't a decision, it's a feeling.
If we could decide who to love, then,
life would be much simpler, but then less magical.

Live 4 d person ho dies 4u,
Smile 4 d person ho cries 4u,
Fight 4 d person ho protects u,
n luv d person ho luvs u more than u..!

When i miss u i read your sms;
when i want to see u i close my eyes,
and

when i want to hear your voice;
I avoid all noise

I have a heart n that is true,
But now it has gone from me to you,
So care for it just like I do,
Because I have no heart n U have two.

24hrs make a lovely day,
7 days make a lovely week,
52 weeks make a lovely year & knowing a person like me will make ur life lovely.
Have a lovely day n life!

Love isn't a decision, it's a feeling.
If we could decide who to love, then,
life would be much simpler, but then less magical.
Those we Love,
Never go away,
They walk beside us everyday Unseen, Unheard,
Still Near,
Still Loved,
Still Missed,
&
Still Very Dear
Just like you..

Wen things go wrong...
Wen sadness fills ur heart...
wen tears flow in ur eyes...

always remember 3 things
1) I'm with u...
2) Still with u...
3) Will ALWAYS b...

When you love someone truly,
you don't look for faults,
you don't look for answers,
you don't look for mistakes.
Instead you fight the mistakes,
you accept the faults and overlook the excuses.

Lives are for living I live for you,
Dreams are for dreaming I dream for you;
Hearts are for beating mine beats for you,
Angels are for keeping. Can I keep you?

Love you more than all the stars in the sky.
I love you more as each moment passes us by.I
love you more with every breath I take.
I love you more with each promise we make.

Love you more than all the stars in the sky.
I love you more as each moment passes us by.I
love you more with every breath I take.
I love you more with each promise we make.

Luv meanz to see someone with closed eyez,
to miss some1 in crowd,
2 find some1 in every thought,
to live 4 some1, luv some1,
but sure tht sum1 is ONLY one!

You are like the sunshine so warm,
you are like sugar, so sweet...
you are like you...
and that's the reason why I love you!

If I could have ,
I would wish to wake up everyday
To the sound of your breath on my neck,
The warmth of your lips on my cheek,
The touch of your fingers on my skin,
And the feel of your heart beating with mine...
Knowing that I could never find that

If I had a penny for everytime I thought of you,
I'd still miss you, but at least I would be rich enough to come and see you..!!

This is a moon which learns from you,
That is a sun which respects you,
There are stars which shine for you,
And here... It's me who lives for you

If Your asking if I Need U the answer is 4Ever..
If Your askin if I'll Leave U the answer is Never..
If Your askin what I value the Answer is U..
if Your askin if I love U the answer is I do.

C.L.I.C.K. means :
C= cant live without u
L= love u
I= i miss u

C= care about u
K= kiss from my heart 2 u
So whenever u miss me just say CLICK.

I dream about you evey night
I shiver when your in sight
I long to hold you close n tight
I wanna be there with all my might
I m just hoping I'm the girl whos right .

I miss you so, here around me, so many people, but yet so alone. I miss your lips, your lovely smile, I miss you each day more and more!

There are a lot of birds wispering only about you, you should once listen to them, then you would know how much I love you.

When i look at you,
i cannot deny there is God,
cause only God could have created some one
as wonderful n beautiful as you.

When the night comes, look at the sky. If you see a falling star, don't wonder why, just make a wish. Trust me, it will come true, 'cause I did it and I found you!

..(>"<)
("(ö,)") A HÜG
..'(.) tö é sé ür stréss

–"""–
(_ _) A KiSS

(_ ö _) tò éasé ür paìn
.-. .-. & my
.'.' .'HÉÄRT
.' . ' tö let U know ì Caré!!

No shadows 2 depress u
only joys 2 surround u
many friends 2 luv u
God himself 2 bless u
These r my wishes 4 u,
for today, tommorrow & everyday.

As days go by, my feelings get stronger,
To be in ur arms, I can't wait any longer.
Look into my eyes & u'll see that it's true,
Day & Night my thought r of U..

Love is like a CD track
That links our hearts together
Dont ever break that CD coz
That wud break my heart too.........

Softly d leaves fo memories wil fal,
i'll pick them up & gather them all,
coz 2day, 2moro & til my life is through
i'll cherish having sum1 like u!

No Life Without Love,
No Answer Without Question???
No Rain Without Cloud....
No Friendship Without
'Y'

'O'
'U'...
MISS U DEAR.......

< Previous   1   2   3   4   5   6   Next >
days go by, my feelings get stronger,
To be in ur arms, I can't wait any longer.
Look into my eyes & u'll see that it's true,
Day & Night my thought r of U..

Softly d leaves fo memories wil fal,
i'll pick them up & gather them all,
coz 2day, 2moro & til my life is through
i'll cherish having sum1 like u!

No Life Without Love,
No Answer Without Question???
No Rain Without Cloud....
No Friendship Without
'Y'
'O'
'U'...
MISS U DEAR.......

Memories r treasured
no1 can steal.
Parting is heartache
no1 can heal.
Sum'll 4get u wen ur gone
but i'll remember u
no matter how long..

I believe that God above created you for me to love. He picked you out from all the rest cause He knew i'd love you the best!

Dear O Dear, ur not near
but i can hear
dont get fear
Ur memories r here
liv wid cheer
no mere tear
and ur mine forever!

Q:Wat is luv?
A:Luv is wen sum1 breaks ur heart
n d most amazing thing
is tat u still luv them
wid every broken piece...!

U may miss me
U may ignore me
U may even forget me
But one day if u wanna c me
Dont search, just c ur shadow
i wil be thr...Trust Me!!

If Your asking if I Need U the answer is 4Ever..
If Your askin if I'll Leave U the answer is Never..
If Your askin what I value the Answer is U..
if Your askin if I love U the answer is I do.

I dream about you evey night
I shiver when your in sight
I long to hold you close n tight
I wanna be there with all my might
I m just hoping I'm the girl whos right .

Red or white
short or tall
wrapped in silver
not wrapped at all
under covers
inside a box
shapes & sizes
love comes in lots.

When i look at you,
i cannot deny there is God,
cause only God could have created some one
as wonderful n beautiful as you .

Ur precious love has
turned my life completely around,
I feel lik Im wlaking but
my feet dont seem 2 touch d ground..!!

if i reached for your hand , will u hold it ?
If i hold out my arms, will u hug me ?
If i go for your lips, will u kiss me ?
If i capture ur heart , will u love me ??

As days go by, my feelings get stronger,
To be in ur arms, I can't wait any longer.

Look into my eyes & u'll see that it's true,
Day & Night my thought r of U..

GOOD MORNING SMS

Treat everyone with politeness,Even those who are rude to U.....Not b coz they are not nice,But bcoz u are nice....!!!**Good morning**

Every bad situation will have something positive...Even a stopped Clock is correct twice a day...Think of this & lead ur life....Good Morning....

Morning is not only sunrise
but a beautiful miracle of GOD
that defeats the darkness & spread light.
May everyday spread light in your whole life.
Amen.
Good Morning

Open ur eyes! So the SUN can rise,Flowers can blossom....Birds can sing,B coz all are waiting to see ur *B*E*A*U*T*I*F*U*L* @S@M@I@L@E@ Good Morning.....

Always ask GOD to give you what you deserve,Not what you desire.Your desires may be few but you deserve a lot.... Good Morning..

Shadows of yesterday
Have faded away,
Sun has reappeared
It's a brand new day
Birds singing their song
Loud and clear,
Announcing to the world
A new day is here,
Sun appears in the east
Has begun a new quest.

,_o/ Pleasant
'l Morning!
./L
CHEER up and REJOICE
Coz every new day brings new Life....
new blessings....
new hope!
Have a nice day! GUD-MORNING!

A Morning is a wonderful blessing,Either stormy or Sunny,It stands for hope,Giving us another start of what we call ...<*L*I*F*E*>...GooD MoRnInG....have A nice dAy.

She is hot !
She is sweet !
She always Needs A lip 4 kiss
Whole world is Mad 4 her !
Who ? Who is she ?
Do you know ?

Answer=Tea
Good morning !!!

Hello,
wake up,
Receive my simple gift of 'GOOD MORNING'
wrapped with sincerity,
tied with care
and
sealed with a prayer
to keep u safe
and
happy all day long!
Take Care!

All mornings are like Paintings:-
U need a little inspiration to get going, a little smile to brighten up & AMS from someone who cares to color ur day...
G@@D M@RNING.....Have a Nice Day..

()""""()
(,□')")
Hi!!
(")(")
Wishing u................
G Morning O Afternoon O Evening D Night
hey, 4 in 1 SMS pack.

The Word 'Hello' means
H=How R U?
E=Everything all right?

L=Like 2 hear 4rm U.
L=Love 2 C U soon.
O=Obviously,
I miss you!
Good Morning my friend.

See outside the Window,
Sun rising for U, Flowers smiling for U,
Birds Singing for U, B'coz last night
I told them to wish U GooD Morning.

Thank you for waking me up.
A warm good morning, after
sweet dreams of last night.
wish you a good day with good morning

We're not too close in distance.
We're not too near in miles.
But text can still touch our hearts
and thoughts can bring us smiles.
Good morning

Happiness is not something u postpone 4 the future.
It"s something u design 4 the present.
Make each moment a happy one.
I just did it by remembering U!
Good Morning & Have a nice day

Hi, now i am coming to meet u...
in the way of sun light...

in the way of sweet breeze...
in the way of good wishes...
just to say good morning...

All mornings are like Paintings:-U need a little inspiration
to get going, a little smile to brighten up & SMS from someone who cares to color ur day...
G@@D M@RNING.....Hav a Nice Day..

Early this morning God gave me 3 baskets of fruits -
LOVE + HAPPINESS + PEACE OF MIND and told me 2 share them with PPL Dear 2 me. I'm sharing all with U...
Good Morning!

Receive my simple gift of Good Morning wrapped with sincerity, Tied with care & sealed with a prayer to keep U safe whole Day!
Good Morning...

No sweet thoughts to forward,no cute graphics to send,just a....TRUE HEART saying...GOOD MORNING

A smile costs less than Electricity,
but gives more light...
Always smile as it is language which everyone understand... So keep smiling
Good morning!

Ooopss...!
...ouch!
(")_(")
) (
(">=<")
_().o.()) ..ohh!
I fell down from d Bed, trying 2 reach 4 my cell.
juz 2 wish u a...
GooD Morning!

Someone never forgets you...
and that is... (put first letter of your name)
=====>>
| V | __|
|_|_|_|__|
Good Morning! Have a nice day!

All mornings are like Paintings:-
U need a little inspiration to get going,
a little smile to brighten up
&
An SMS from someone who cares to color ur day...
Good Morning

Morning time a cup of hot hello,
A plate of crispy wishes,
A spoon of sweet smiles &
A slice of great success specially for u...
Enjoy the day!!!!!!!!
"Good Morning"

Sending u 1000 smiles take 1 for now &
Keep the remaining 999 under ur pillow,
Pick out 1 every morning coz
I want 2 see u smiling always. Good Morning

?It is a
S"imple"
M"ind touching"
I"nteractive"
L"ong lasting"
E"ffect which Wins the hearts..
Yes..Its your "SWEET SMILE"
So Keep smiling always, good morning!

As I open my eyes, I thank God for allowing me to see a new day & to greet a Sweet friend like U! Gud Morning!

Morning greetings doesn't only mean saying Good Morning, it has a silent message saying: I remember you when I wake up! Have a nice day!

Extending One Hand to Help Somebody has More Value, than Joining Two Hands for Prayer. Gud Morning.

An honest smile, smiled from a smiling heart, crossing miles apart, has just reached ur inbox to wish u a day full of smiles & happiness. Gud Day!

I requested the sun to rise early and requested god to make your day healthy. Good morning

Squeeze the past like a sponge, smell the present like a rose, and send a kiss to the future. Gud Day!

Your soul came back from dreamland reunited with a sleeping senseless piece of yourself. Slowly open ur eyes realise it's a brand new day. Good Morning.

The world doesnot need more mountains to climb,More seas to cross,or more stars to shine, What the world needs is only more of U & UR smile!! GOOD MORNING.

The Breeze has awakened the Earth & the Sun has coloured our world. The birds have added melody to the morning & I hope I'm not late to wish U Gud Morning.

GOODNIGHT SMS

If u feel little bored,little sick,little sad,all lost,
U know whats wrong?
U r suffering from lack of Vitamin 'ME'

One evening i will come 2 ur room
lock the door, turn off the lights, join u in bed
I'll come closer 2 u, my lips near ur face
And I'll shout, Have a gr8 night!!!

A shining ANGEL stands beside your silky bed,
Calling ur nice Name so softly,
Throwing flowers on U
And saying Good Night & Sweet Dreams.

Good night my very special friend,
I pray you lay in rest,
And may tomorrow bring you
Much love and happiness.
Do not think of me…i m in ur eyes, in ur heart

Art of living:
First of all,dont make friends.
if made,dont go close to them.
if gone,dont like them.
if liked,then plz.. dont leave them.
Good Night, sweet dreams…

Never blame a day in ur life.
Good days give u happiness.
Bad days give u experience.
Both are essential in life!
All are Gods blessings!
good night.

Do not count what u have lost.
Just see what u have now,
because past never comes back
but sometimes future can give
u back ur lost things! 'good night'.

somewhere out there beneath the pale moon light someone think in of u some where out there where dreams come true... goodnite & sweet dreams 2 you.

As u go 2 bed 2night, I ordered bats 2 guard u tight. I told some ghosts to dance in white & 2 make sure u r alryt, I'll ask the Dracula 2 kiss ur neck goodnight..

My day may be hectic. My schedule may be tight.
But I would never let the day end without saying good night.
Sweet dreams...

Money can buy a house not home,
A bed but not sleep, medicine but not health,
Money is dirty, it only cause pain & suffering.
SEND me all UR MONEY & BE HAPPY.

1 2 3 4 5 6
hide my tears when I say ur name, But the pain in my heart is still the same. Although I smile & seem carefree, there's no one who miss U more than me.

Dont ever give up when you are down..
it doesnt matter if u fall many tyms..
just remember that each time u fall ..
i'll nvr let u reach d ground..

trust me..i'll always be around.
gudnite..

Dont ever give up wen u r down..it doesnt matter if u fall many tyms..jst remember that each time u fall ..il nvr let u reach d ground..trust me..il always be around.gudnyt..

The greatest gift u can give 2 sum1 is your time.
B'coz when u give sum1 ur time.
You're givin them a portion of life that U never get back.

Whenever you have a DREAM inside your HEART,
Never let it go coz DREAMS are the TINY SEEDS,
From which BEAUTIFUL TOMORROW GROWS
Have a wonderful dream tonight?

A day is going to end again.
It is nice to have a friend like U
making my everyday seems so great.
Thank U my good friend lastly
good night n sweet dreams…

On this cold cold nite,in My small small ROOm,i Look At The Brite Brite StArS iN tHe DaRk DaRk sKy & DrEaM of YouR sWeet sWeet SmiLe on ur CuTe CuTe FaCe! GdNiTe

Wash your face and wash your feet! Now itz time 2 fall asleep. Yours eyes are weak N mouth can't speak so hope tis nite shall b nice and sweet. Good Nite.

Stars light Stars bright u're the only Star I see tonight. I wish I may. I wish I might be there guarding ur dreams tonite, gd nite sweet dreams.

Good night my very special friend,I pray you lay in rest,And may tomorrow bring you,Much love and happiness.
do not think of me...i m in ur eyes.
Posted by: Moderator

A special face,a special smile, a special someone, a special hug from me to u, a special person, I found in u, Sweet Dreams, Sleep well!
Good Night Sms
ThinGs 2 TaKe NoTe WheN u SleeP: 1st-MiSS Me, 2nd-ThInk oF ME, 3rd-HuG Me, 4th-LoVE mE. TrY 2 SLEEp NoW & ClOSe Ur EyeS. Get PrePaReD 2 DrEaM oF mE! Good Night.

Take a deep breath,
Stand near the window,
Look at the sky,
There will be two stars twinkling brightly,
u know what they are????
They are my eyes always taking care of U..
Good night.

wish that God would hold u tite. i hope that angels will keep u in site. Now just2make sure u feel all rite, i'm gonna wish u a wonderful nite! sleep tite.

Despite the Old saying "Don't Take Your Troubless & Worries To Bed" Most of the People still sleep with their wives!!! WHAT A CRAZY WORLD, Good Night.

We've been thru a path so dark,
but we stil gotten dat special spark,
now we noe dat we can neva go rong,
my luv fer u wil neva b gone.

Touch ur heart;
Close ur eyes;
Make a wish;
Say GoodNight;
Sky so wide,
Stars so bright,
Turn off the lights,
and say Good Night....

Hey u!!! Yes u... the cute one... holding this phone! are you asleep? Juste wanted 2 say Good Night..!

sleepy msg for a sleepy person
from a sleepy friend
for a sleepy reason
at a sleepy time

on the sleepy day
in a sleepy mood
to say please sleep
"good night"

Saying gudnite is not just putting
an end to a day.Its a way of saying ,
I remember u before i go 2 sleep.
Hope u can fel the care that goes with it....
GOOD NIGHT..

The night is silent but I can't sleep. Maybe because I am waiting for my cell phone to beep. Before I dream, what I want is get your message and read.

Let ur eye lashes hug each other for few hours.
Happy journey into the world of dreams..
GOOD NIGHT !
Welcome aboard2 "Sweet Dreams" airline,
All passengers on bed, hug ur pillows
As the flight will be leaving soon 2dream land.
Enjoy ur time GOOD'NITE!

12'.9!/3'.6.'.'12'.9!_3'.6.'.'12'.9 _!3'.6.' still awake? Time to sleep, GOOD NITE+SLEEP TIGHT+SWEET DREAMZ!!!

Notice ur phone got heavier with this message ? it contains load of love. affection and prayers to keep u happy n safe. Have a nive sleep Good nite!

0 0 0 0 .shhhhhhhhh.I'm walking slowly,bcoz u might be sleeping,I'll just leave my message 4u"GOOD NIGHT & SWEET DREAMS.

Hello ! This is our ATD
(Any Time Disturbance) service.
We are the experts in disturbing
and irritating people at busy hours.
Our goal has been achieved.
Thank you!... "Good Night"

Sun wouldn't be red,
Sea wouldn't be blue,
I wouldn't be happy,
Without disturbing you!.
"Goodnight"

On this night as i lie on my bed,i just cant stop thinking about u my LOVE.May u have a blessed & a beatiful GUD NITE.

Goodnight!
Here r 1000 Gud N8 Kisses 4U, take 1 now put d other 999 under ur pillow. Gdn8!

Have a
"salt Dreamz..."
Bcoz daily sweet is not
Good for U'r health,take care....

Night doesnt become beautiful with star studded sky & full moon,It becomes beautiful when

u go to sleep
and let stars & moon admire ur innocence..Good night

U r the reason for my sleepless nights. U r the reason why I tend to hold my pillow tight. It's u that I'm thinking of when I lay down at night. And u r thereason I can't sleep without sayin Gudnight.

Night is a wonderful opportunity to take rest, to forgive, to dream, to smile and to get ready for all the battle that you have to fight tomorrow. Good Night

Night is longer than day for those who DREAM & day is longer than night for those who make their DREAMS come true. Wish you Good Night & Sweet Dreams

Wash ur face and wash ur feet! Now it's time 2 fall asleep. Your eyes are weak and mouth can't speak so, hope this nite shall b nice n sweet. Good Night.

No matter if the sky is black or blue.. No matter .. If there are stars or moon.. As long as ur heart is true.. Sweet dreams will always be with u. Gud Night!

Love sweet as sugar, bitter if you dont know it better.bed the best place to think of memories which put u to sleep,telling u goodnite.

On this night as i lie on my bed,i just cant stop thinking about u my LOVE.May u have a blessed & a beatiful
GUD NITE.

Night doesnt become beautiful with star studded sky & full moon,It becomes beautiful when u go to sleep and let stars & moon admire ur innocence..Good night.

Night is a wonderful opportunity to take rest, to forgive, to dream, to smile and to get ready for all the battle that you have to fight tomorrow. Gud Night.

ACRONYMS & ABBREVIATIONS

Acronyms, abbreviations, mnemonics and bacronyms for amusement

Acronyms, whether true acronyms or not, and abbreviations, add colour, fun and interest to our language. They are also memory devices. They act as 'short-hand' and increase the efficiency of communications: meaning is conveyed in less time and fewer words.

A3	Any time, Any place, Anywhere..
A2O	Apples To Oranges. Acronym to highlight any inappropriate comparison; a modern shorthand for 'chalk and cheese'.
AAA	Alive, Alert, Aggressive.
ABC	Always Be Closing.
ABCD	Above and Beyond the Call of Duty. Also American Born Confused Desi
ACT	Action Conquers Terror.
ADDIE	Analysis, Design, Development, Implementation, Evaluation.
AFLO	Another Flipping Learning Opportunity. A big mistake or onerous task.

AFOL	All Fine On Leaving.
AFTO	Ask For The Order.
AIDA	Attention, Interest, Desire, Action.
AKA	Also Known As..
ALF	Always Listen First.
ALO	A Learning Opportunity.
AMAT	All Mouth And Trousers.
AOX3	Alert, Oriented times 3 (person, place, time).
APB	All-Points Bulletin.
APE	Attentive, Peripheral, Empathic.
ART	Assuming Room Temperature.
ASBO	Anti-Social Behaviour Order.
ASDA	Age, Site, Depth, Area.
ASK	Activity, Skills, Knowledge.
ASTRO	Always Stating The Really Obvious.
ATNA	All Talk No Action.
AWOL	Absent Without Leave.
AVPU	Alert, Voice, Pain, Unresponsive.
AWTF	Away With The Fairies.
B2B	Business To Business.
B2C	Business To Consumer
B2G	Business To Government
B2E	Business To Everybody

B2A	Business To Anybody
B2B2C	Business To Business To Consumer.
BANANA	Built Absolutely Nothing Anywhere Near Anyone.
BANJO	Bang Another Nuisance Job Out.
BAU	Business As Usual.
BDU	Brain Dead User.
BEER	Behaviour, Effect, Expectation, Results.
BENDWIMP	Beliefs, Evidence, Needs, Desires, Wounds, Interests, Mentors, Proud of.
BFI	Brute Force and Ignorance.
BIAT	Boss Is A Twit/Twerp/Twat etc.
BID	Break It Down.
BITCH	Babe In Total Control of Herself.
BLT	Base-Line Test.
BLUF	Bottom Line Up Front.
BMT	Before My Time.
BOB	Battery Operated Boyfriend.
BOBO	Burnt Out But Opulent.
BOCCA	Belief, Optimism, Courage, Conviction, Action.
BOGOFF	Buy One Get One For Free.

BOOSTER	Balanced, Observed, Objective, Specific, Timely, Enhancing, Relevant..
BPO	Business Process Outsourcing.
BRAN	Benefits, Risks, Alternatives, Nothing.
BRIC	Brazil, Russia, India, China.
BTW	By The Way.
BURP	Bankrupt Unemployed Rejected Person.
BYO	Bring Your Own Booze/Bottle.
CADET	Can't Add, Doesn't Even Try.
CAP	Cover All Possibilities.
CARAT	Counselling, Advice, Referral, Assessment and Throughcare.
CASH	Computer Assisted Self-Help.
CHAOS	Chief Has Arrived On Scene.
CHIP	Come Home I'm Pregnant.
CLM	Career Limiting Move.
CRAFT	Can't Remember A Flipping Thing.
CSN	Computer Says No.

CSR	Corporate Social Responsibility.
CT	Cerca Trova. Italian, meaning 'He who seeks, finds'
CTD	Circling the Drain. \ Close To Death.
C**T	Computer User Non-Technical.
DAGMAR	Defining Advertising Goals for Measured Advertising Results.
DELTA	Doesn't Ever Leave The Airport.
DIAGEO	Don't Imagine Any Great Employment Opportunities.
DIARRHOEA	Dash In A Real Rush, Hurry Or Else Accident.
DIF (analysis)	Difficulty, Importance, Frequency.
DIKWIAD?	Do I Know What I Am Doing?
DIMWIT	Don't Interrupt Me While I'm Talking.
DIN	Do It Now.
DINA	Description Is Not Analysis.
DINK/DINKY	Double Income No Kids/Yet.

DITCHED	Dual Income, Two Children, Expanding Debts.
DMAIC	Define opportunity, Measure performance, Analyse opportunity, Improve performance, Control performance.
DREAM	Dedication, Responsibility, Education, Attitude, Motivation.
DRIB	Don't Read If Busy.
DRIVE	Define, Review, Identify, Verify, Execute.
DRIVER	Documents, Records, Interviews, Visuals, Evaluation, Review.
DRM	Digital Rights Management..
DRT	Dead Right There.
DTS	Danger To Shipping.
DUTCHIE	Defer Until The Christmas Holiday Is Ended.
E&OE	Errors and Omissions Excepted.
EDIP	Explain, Demonstrate, Imitate, Practice.
EFTPOS	Electronic Funds Transfer at Point Of Sale.
EGYPT	Eager To Grab Your Pretty Toes

EPACA	Evaluate, Plan, Action, Check, Amend.
EPOS	Electronic Point Of Sale.
ETAM	Everything To Attract Men.
FAB	Features, Advantages, Benefits.
FAS	Fat And Stupid.
FEAR	Forget Everything And Run.
FIDO	Forget It and Drive On.
FIFO	First In First Out.
FILO	First In Last Out.
FIGS	French, Italian, German, Spanish.
FINE	Fanatical, Insecure, Neurotic and Emotional.
FIRE	Find Inform Restrict Extinguish.
FISH	First In Stays Here.
FISH & CHIPS	Fighting In Someone's House & Causing Havoc In People's Streets.
FIST	First In Stays There.
FLK	Funny Looking Kid.
FLKFLP	Funny Looking Kid, Funny Looking Parents.
FLUF	Fat Little Ugly Fellow.
FMCG	Fast Moving Consumer Goods.

FOAK	First Of A Kind..
FOBIO	Frequently Outwitted By Inanimate Objects.
FOC	Free Of Charge.
FOCUS(ED)	Futuristic Observation Creates Unique Solutions (Enabling Development).
FOOSH	Fall On Out-Stretched Hand.
FORCE	Focus On Reducing Costs Everywhere.
FORD	Found On Roadside, Dead..
FRED	Flipping Ridiculous Electronic Device.
FUCT	Failed Under Continuous Testing.
FUD	Fear, Uncertainty and Doubt.
GAAFOFY	Go Away And Find Out For Yourself.
GAAP	Generally Accepted Accounting Principles.
GAAS	Generally Accepted Auditing Standards.
GAK	God Alone Knows.
GASP	Group Against Smokers Pollution.
GIGO	Garbage In Garbage Out.
GLM	Good Looking Mum.

GLAM	Greying, Leisured, Affluent, Married.
GMC	Garbage Made Carefully.
GOAT	Greatest Of All Time.
GOCO	Government Owned, Contractor Operated.
GOK	God Only Knows.
GOLF	Gentlemen Only, Ladies Forbidden.
GOSPA	Goals, Objectives, Strategies, Plans, Activities.
GPO	Good for Parts Only.
GROW	Goals, Reality, Options, Will.
GUBU	Grotesque, Unbelievable, Bizarre, and Unprecedented.
GWR	Goes When Ready.
HCM	Human Capital Management.
HIV	Hair Is Vanishing.
HIVI	Husband Is Village Idiot.
HOLLAND	Our Love Lasts And Never Dies.
HOPEFUL	Hard-up Old Person Expecting Full Useful Life.
HTH	Hope This Helps.
HTML	How To Make Love.
IAMS	It's About Me Stupid.

IBM	I Blame Microsoft/ I've Been Married/ Idiots Become Managers.
ICE	In Case of Emergency.
IDEA	Identify, Design, Execute, Augment.
IIP	Investors In People.
IKIWISI	I'll Know It When I See It.
IKWIWWISI	I'll Know What I Want When I See It.
IMCIS	Identify, Manage, Change, Improve, Show.
IMHO	In My Humble Opinion.
INSET	In-Service Education and Training.
IOWA	Idiots Out Walking About (or Wandering Around).
IP	Intellectual Property.
ITALY	I Trust And Love You.
JIT	Just In Time.
JOB	Just Over Broke.
KAS	Knowledge, Attitude, Skills.
KASH	Knowledge, Attitude, Skills, Habits.
KEV	Key Ethical Value.
KEY	Keep Extending Yourself.
KISS	Keep It Simple Stupid.
KPI/KSI	Key Performance Indicator/ Key Success Indictor.

LADIES	Life After Divorce Is Eventually Saner.
LAMP	Lower Academically-Minded Person.
LANO	Lights Are Not On.
LAST	Listen, Advise, Solve, Thank.
LEAR	Listen, Empathise, Ask, Resolve.
LEDO	Listen, Empathise, De-personalise, Offer.
LIFER	Lazy Ignorant Fool Expecting Retirement.
LIP	Low Involvement Product.
LITE	Load, Individual, Task/Travel, Environment.
LOBNAH	Lights On But Nobody's At Home.
LOL	Lots of Love. (Or) Laughing Out Loud.
LONI	Lights On, Nobody In.
MAAH	Mad As A Hatter.
MAEW	Moves All Extremities Well.
MBWA	Management By Walking Around/Wandering About.
MECE	Mutually Exclusive, Comprehensively Exhaustive.
MEGO	My Eyes Glazed Over.

MELVIN	Mediocrity, Ego, Limits, Vanity, Incompetence, Name-calling.
MILE	Maximum Impact, Little Effort.
MIP	Mobility Impaired Person.
MMM or 3M	Measurable, Manageable, Motivational.
MOLAD	Matter Of Life And Death.
MOP	Measure Of Performance.
MTBCM	Mean Time Between Changes of Mind.
MUPPIE	Middle-aged Urban Professional.
NALGO	Not A Lot Going On.
NATO	Not A Team Operator/No Action, Talk Only/ Not A Team Operator
NEET	Not in Employment, Education or Training.
NIGY	Now I've Got You.
NIGHTMARE	Negative, Ignorant, Greedy, Hopeless, Thankless, Miserable, Angry, Rude, Envious.
NINJA	No Income, No Job or Assets..
NQR	Not Quite Right.
NSFW	Not Safe For Work.
OAP	Over Anxious Person.

OGRO	O Great Responsible One.
OINKY	One Income, No Kids Yet.
OOO	Out of office
ORCHID	One Recent Child, Heavily In Debt.
PAL	Phase Alternate Line.
PANIC	Pressured And Not In Control.
PAY	Prioritise Activities by Yield.
PCMCIA	People Can't Memorise Computer Industry Acronyms.
PDA	Public Display of Affection.
PDQ	Pretty Damn Quick. Or Pretty Darned Quick.
PEP	Paternalistic, Economic, Participative.
PEST	Political, Economic, Social, Technological.
PICNIC	Problem In Chair Not In Computer.
PIG	Pride, Integrity and Guts.
PINS	Persons In Need of Supervision.
PISA	Permanent and Irrecoverable State of Alcoholism.
PLMK	Please Let Me Know.
PLU	People Like Us.

POETS (day)	Push Off Early, Tomorrow's Saturday.
POS	Point Of Sale.
POV	Point Of View.
PPPP or The Four P's	Product, Price, Promotion, Place.
PRIC	Problem, Rectification, Investigation, Correction.
PRIDE	Personal Responsibility In Delivering Excellence.
RABADAD	Running A Business And Doing A Degree.
RAPC	Run Away People Coming.
RFI	Request For Information.
RFP	Request For Proposal.
RHINO	Really Here In Name Only.
ROI	Return On Investment.
ROMEO	Retired Old Men Eating Out.
RORO	Roll On Roll Off.
ROTFLA..	Rolling On The Floor Laughing And...
RPM	Resale Price Maintenance.
RTQ2	Read The Question Twice.
RUB	Rich Urban Biker.
SABENA	Such A Bad Experience, Never Again.
SADFAB	Single And Desperate For A Baby.
SATs	Stupid Ass Test(s).

SEP	Someone Else's Problem.
SHOT IT	Should Have Ordered This In Time.
SINA	Safety Is No Accident.
SINBAD	Single Income No Boyfriend And Desperate.
SINOAP	Solution In Need Of A Problem.
SITCOM	Single Income Two Children Oppressive Mortgage.
SKI-ing	Spending the Kids' Inheritance.
SLEPT	Social, Legal, Economic, Political, Technological.
SMART	Specific, Measurable, Agreed, Realistic, Time-bound.
SMARTER	Specific, Measurable, Agreed, Realistic, Time-bound, Ethical, Recorded.
SMOP	Simple Matter Of Programming.
SNERT	Snot-Nosed Egotistical Rude Teenager.
SOAR/SOA	Situation, Opportunity, Action, Result.
SOGI	Situation, Opportunity, Action, Result, (Reflect). tch.) (Ack DC)

SOHO	Senior Officer's Good Idea.
SONTTAP	Small Office/Home Office.
SOS	Say Only Nice Things To All People.
SPC	Save Our Souls.
SPECTRUM	Statistical Process Control.
SPEW	Silly People Expect Computers To Replace Useless Managers.
SPOF	Single Person Evaluation Worksheet.
SPOH	Single Point Of Failure.
SQ3R	Safe Pair Of Hands.
STEPPPA	Survey, Question, Read, Recall, Review.
STM	Subject, Target, Emotion.
SUMO	Shut Up Move On.
SWMBO ('swambo')	She Who Must Be Obeyed.
SWALK	Sealed With A Loving Kiss.
SWAN	Sell What's Available Now.
SWOT	Strengths, Weaknesses, Opportunities, Threats.
TAPES	Technique And Practice (or Pressure) Equals Skill.
TANSTAAFL	There Ain't No Such Thing As A Free Lunch.
TARDIS	Time And Relative Dimensions In Space.
TATT	Tired All The Time..

T-CUP	Total Control Under Pressure/ Think Correctly Under Pressure/ Thinking Clearly Under Pressure
TEAM	Together Everyone Achieves More.
TEETH	Tried Everything Else?.. Try Homeopathy.
TED	Tell me, Explain to me, Describe to me.
TEPID	Tastes Expensive, Pension Inadequate, Dammit.
TGIF	Thank God It's Friday.
THICK	Those Having Insufficient Cerebral Kinesis.
TIC	Taken Into Consideration.
TIP	Theory Into Practice.
TINA	There Is No Alternative.
TLA	Three Letter Acronym.
TLAR	That Looks About Right. Thanks, but No Thanks. Think Outside The Box/ Thinking Outside The Box.
TOTBAL	There Ought To Be A Law
TPTB	The Powers That Be.
TQC	Total Quality Control. Forerunning theory from the 1970s to TQM, and successor to SPC..
TQM	Total Quality Management.

TQMS	Total Quality Management System.
TRIP	Transaction, Relationship, Information, Partnership.
TTFN	Ta Ta For Now.
TTS and CCC	Teams, Tools, Systems and Culture, Communication, Commitment.
TWAIN	Technology Without An Interesting Name.
TWOC	Taking Without Owner's Consent.
UMBRO	yoU Must Be Really Old.
UPB	Unique Perceived Benefit.
USP	Unique Selling Point (or Proposition).
VEST	Very Egotistical Stupid Twit.
VIOT	Village Idiot On Tour.
WAFI	Wind Assisted Flaming Idiot.
WDIS	Where Do I Sign?
WHY	What Have You.
WIIFM	What's In It For Me?
WINDOWS	Will Install Needless Data On Whole System. Classic ironic 'backronym'. Perhaps a little unfair, but need we say more?...
WLOG	Without Loss Of Generality.

WOMBAT	Waste Of Money, Brains And Time.
WOOF	Well Off Older Folk.
WOOO	We're On Our Own.
WOOP	Well Off Older Person.
WOTCHA	Wonderful Old Thing Considering His/Her Age.
WRAP	Wind, Reel And Print.
WYSBYGI	What You See Before You Get It.
WYSIWYG	What You See Is What You Get.
WYGIWYD	What You Get Is What You Deserve.
YAHOO	You Always Have Other Options.
YAVIS	Young, Attractive, Verbal, Intelligent, Successful.
YMMV	Your Mileage Might Vary/ Your Mileage May Vary.
YOYO	You're On Your Own.
YUPPIE	Young Upwardly-mobile Professional.
BURP	Bankrupt Unemployed Rejected Person.
DINKY	Double Income No Kids Yet.
GLAM	Greying, Leisured, Affluent, Married.
KIPPERS	Kids In Parents' Pockets Eroding Retirement Savings.

LOMBARD	Loads Of Money But A Real Donut/Dickhead.
LIFER	Lazy Ignorant Fool Expecting Retirement.
MUPPIE	Middle-aged Urban Professional.
NEET	Not in Employment, Education or Training.
NINJA	No Income, No Job or Assets.
OINKY	One Income, No Kids Yet.
ORCHID	One Recent Child, Heavily In Debt.
RABADAD	Running A Business And Doing A Degree.
ROB	Rich Ordinary Briton.
ROMEO	Retired/Rich/Respectable Old Men Eating Out/Enjoying Outings.
RUB	Rich Urban Biker.
SADFAB	Single And Desperate For A Baby.
SAL	Suburban Asset Lightweight.
SINBAD	Single Income No Boyfriend And Desperate.
SITCOM	Single Income Two Children Oppressive Mortgage.
SKI-ing	Spending the Kids' Inheritance.

SNAG	Sensitive New-Age Guy.
SNERT	Snot-Nosed Egostical Rude Teenager.
SPOOLA/SPOOLAs	Stripped Pine, Olive Oil, Laura Ashley.
TEPID	Tastes Expensive, Pension Inadequate, Dammit.
VEST	Very Egotistical Stupid Twit.
WASP	White Anglo-Saxon Protestant.
WOOF	Well Off Older Folk.
WOOP	Well Off Older Person.
WOTCHA	Wonderful Old Thing Considering His/Her Age.
YUPPIE	Young Upwardly-mobile Professional.
AWOL	All Well On Leaving.
AWTF	Away With The Fairies.
DTS	Danger To Shipping.
DRT	Dead Right There
DRTTTT	Dead Right There, There, There, and There.
FAS	Fat And Stupid.
FDGB	Fall Down Go Boom.
FLK	Funny Looking Kid. Funny Looking Kid, Funny Looking Parents.
FOOSH	Fall On Out-Stretched Hand.

GAK	God Alone Knows.
GBC	General Body Crumble.
GLM	Good Looking Mum.
GOK	God Only Knows.
GOMER	Get Out of My Emergency Room.
GPO	Good for Parts Only.
GROLIES	Guardian Reader Of Limited Intelligence, Ethnic Skirt.
HIVI	Husband Is Village Idiot.
MAAH	Mad As A Hatter.
NKDA	No Known Drug Allergies. Alternatively the abbreviation is used to mean Not Known, Didn't Ask.
NOONG	Not One Of Nature's Gentlemen.
NQR	Not Quite Right.
NYDN	Not Yet Diagnosed - Nervous.
OAP	Over Anxious Person.
PEARL	Pupils Equal And Reacting To Light.
PERRLA	Pupils Equal, Round, Reactive to Light and Accommodate to distance.
PISA	Permanent and Irrecoverable State of Alcoholism.

RICE	Rest, Ice, Compression, Elevation.
SOB	Shortness Of Breath.
TATT	Tired All The Time.
TEETH	Tried Everything Else?.. Try Homeopathy.
TOBASH	Take Out Back And Shoot.
YAHOO	You Always Have Other Options.

CHRISTMAS SMS

If one night a big fat man jumps in at your window grabs you and puts you in a sack do not worry I told Santa I wanted you for CHRISTMAS

May the joy and peace of Christmas be with you all through the Year. Wishing you a season of blessings from heaven above.

Happy Christmas

May the good times and treasures of the present become the golden memories of tomorrow. Wish you lots of love, joy and happiness. MERRY CHRISTMAS

May your world be filled with warmth and good cheer this Holy season, and throughout the year. Wish your christmas be filled with peace and love. Merry X-mas

I am dreaming of a white Christmas, with every christmas card i write, May your days be merry and bright, and May all your christmases be white. Happy Christmas.

I hope you have a wonderful christmas .

have a great new year.

Hopefully santa will be extra good to you . enjoy your holidays.

If one night you wake up and a big fat male is trying to put you in a sack please dont be afraid because i told santa all i want for christmas is you.

Lets welcome the year which is fresh and new, Lets cherish each moment it beholds, Lets celebrate this blissful New Year. Merry X-mas

New is the year, new are the hopes

New is the year, new are the hopes and the aspirations, new is the resolution, new are the spirits and forever my warm wishes are for u.Have a promising and fulfilling new year.

Blessed is the season which engages the whole world in a conspiracy of love.

May your world be filled with warmth and good cheer this Holy season, and throughout the year.Wish your christmas be filled with peace and love. Merry X-mas.

Christmas may be many things

or it may be a few.

For you, the joy

is each new toy;

for me;

its watching U.

Two things upon this changing earth can neither change nor end; the splendor of Christ's humble birth, the love of friend for friend.

Ur friendship is a glowing ember through the yr n each december frm its warm n livin spark v kindle flame against da dark n with its shining radiance light our tree of faith on Christmas night.

May all the sweet magic

Of Christmas conspire

To gladden your hearts

And fill every desire.

Lets welcome the year which is fresh and new,Lets cherish each moment it beholds, Lets celebrate this blissful New year. Merry X-mas.

Can I have your picture, so Santa Claus knows exactly what to give me. Happy Christmas.

An occasion that is celebrated as a reflection of your values, desires, affections, traditions.

Heap on the wood!-the wind is chill; But let it whistle as it will, Well keep our Christmas merry still.

Christmas waves a magic wand over this world, and behold, everything is softer and more beautiful.

Jingle bells Jingle bells what fun it is to wish our friends a very Merry Christmas.

Bells are ringing the wishes of christmas day the flying snowflakes send my most sincere blessings to you. Merry Christmas.

- **Dont** expect too much of Christmas Day. You can't crowd into it any arrears of unselfishness and kindliness that may have accrued during the past twelve months.
- **Bless** us Lord, this Christmas, with quietness of mind; Teach us to be patient and always to be kind.
- **Christmas** is not a time nor a season, but a state of mind. To cherish peace and goodwill, to be plenteous in mercy, is to have the real spirit of Christmas.
- **There** is no ideal Christmas; only the one Christmas you decide to make as a reflection of your values, desires, affections, traditions.
- **Joy** resounds in the hearts of those who believe in the miracle of Christmas.
- **Wishing** you all the peace, joy, and love of the season, Seasons Greetings.
- **Somehow**, not only for Christmas, But all the long year through, The joy that you give to others, is the joy that comes back to you. And the more you spend in blessing, The poor and lonely and sad, The more of your hearts possessing, Returns to you glad.
- **Faith** makes all things possible. Hope makes all things work. Love makes all things beautiful. May you have all the three for this Christmas.

MERRY CHRISTMAS... MORE

Bells are ringing the wishes of christmas day the flying snowflakes send my most sincere blessings to you merry christmas.

Christmas

Jingle bells Jingle bells what fun it is to wish our friends a very merry christmas.

May your world be filled with warmth and good chear this Holy season, and throughout the year. Wish your christmas be filled with peace and love. Merry X-mas.

May the joy and peace of Christmas be with you all through the Year. Wishing you a season of blessings from heaven above. Happy Christmas.

Christmas is the season for kindling the fire of hospitality in the hall, the genial flame of charity in the heart.

A Christmas candle is a lovely thing; It makes no noise at all, But softly gives itself away; While quite unselfish, it grows small.

Lets welcome the year which is fresh and new, Lets cherish each moment it beholds, Lets celebrate this blissful New year. Merry X-mas.

From Home to home, and heart to heart, from one place to another. The warmth and joy of Christmas, brings us closer to each other.

A silent night, a star above, a blessed gift of hope and love. A blessed Christmas to you.

NEW YEAR SMS

Years come n go, but this year I specially wish 4 u a double dose of health n happiness topped with loads of good fortune. Have a gr8 year ahead! HAPPY NEW YEAR.

Oh my Dear, Forget ur Fear,
Let all ur Dreams be Clear,
Never put Tear, Please Hear,
I want to tell one thing in ur Ear
Wishing u a very Happy "NEW YEAR"!

Like birds, let us, leave behind what we don't need to carry…
GRUDGES SADNESS PAIN FEAR and REGRETS.
Life is beautiful, Enjoy it. HAPPY NEW YEAR

Nights are Dark but Days are Light,
Nights are Dark but Days are Light,
Wish your Life will always be Bright.
So my Dear don't get Fear
Coz, God Gift us a BRAND NEW YEAR.
HAPPY NEW YEAR…

Beauty..
Freshness..
Dreams..
Truth..
Imagination..
Feeling..
Faith..

Trust..
This is begining of a new year.

New Year is the time to unfold new horizons
& realize new dreams,
to rediscover the strength
& faith within u,
to rejoice in simple pleasures
& gear up 4 a new challenges.
Wishing u a truly fulfilling Happy New Year.

Little keys open big locks
Simple words reflect great thoughts
Your smile can cure heart blocks
So keep on smiling it rocks.
Happy New Year 2008.